DREAMLAND

The Inside Story of the '93-'94 Houston Rockets' Championship Season

D1571986

DreamLand

The Inside Story of the '93-'94 Houston Rockets' Championship Season

Robert Falkoff

Foreword by Rudy Tomjanovich

Gulf Publishing Company
Houston, Texas

To Jackie, Joey, Laurie, Mama and Daddy,
my champions of the world.

DREAMLAND

Gulf Publishing Company
Book Division
P.O. Box 2608 ☐ Houston, Texas 77252-2608

10   9   8   7   6   5   4   3   2   1

Library of Congress Cataloging-in-Publication Data

Falkoff, Robert, 1952–
    Dreamland : the inside story of the Houston Rockets' 1994 championship season / Robert Falkoff.
        p.   cm.
    ISBN 0-88415-251-0
    1. Houston Rockets (Basketball team)— History.   I. Title.
GV885.52.H68F35   1994
796.323'64'097641411—dc20   94-31682
                                                          CIP

Contents

Foreword

To be a part of Houston's first major sports championship . . . it's like a fairy tale.

Especially with my background as a guy who came to Houston with the Rockets in the early 1970s and worked my way through the organization, which I always felt was a privilege.

I've spent many years in this city—working for the Rockets and being a fan of the Oilers and Astros. To be the head coach and get the big payoff—not only for the Rockets but for the whole city—I wish I had all the words to describe my feelings.

I felt this team learned how to win in '92–'93 and then had a great carryover to '93–'94. We added some key players and conquered some pressure situations in the regular season.

A big factor in winning this championship was what happened to us after losing the first two games of the Phoenix series at home. Sometimes, it takes something very negative to trigger something very positive. That experience got us to the core of who we really were, and I've never been prouder than when we won those two games in Phoenix to even that series.

Reading this book really brought back the excitement and enabled me to re-live a season that will always be extra special. When you are going through it as a coach, you just go about your job from day to day, trying to win the next game. You don't look back and you don't look too far ahead.

But now, we can look back and take pride in something we'll savor the rest of our lives. It's easy to get carried away after the fact, but this book reminds me of what a long, hard-fought battle it was to get to the top—sometimes I even ask myself, "How the heck could we have done that?"

For the Rockets to become world champions, it took a remarkable collective effort on the part of the players, the coaching staff, the entire organization, and our great fans.

It's like a dream . . . but most dreams aren't this good.

Rudy Tomjanovich
Head Coach, Houston Rockets

I don't worry so much about reaching the destination. The key in life is to enjoy the journey.

Houston Rockets center Hakeem Olajuwon

Preface

In the year of The Dream, why not do as Hakeem Olajuwon suggests?

The purpose of this book is to enjoy the 1993–94 Houston Rockets' journey to a history-making first major world championship for a Houston sports team.

Coming off a strong finish in '92–'93, I thought there was a chance of Houston going all the way. Not a great chance, but a chance.

I decided to file daily notes in a journal so that if the Rockets were to make it to the NBA mountaintop, that journal of the inner-workings of the team—along with excerpts from my daily newspaper writings in *The Houston Post*—would give fans a keener appreciation of the arduous nine-month struggle that a team must endure to win a world championship.

Sometimes, truth is indeed stranger than fiction.

For anyone who has seen the movie *Major League*—about a gutsy ballclub made up of diverse personalities that somehow banded together and won despite some bizarre front-office happenings—this Rockets' saga may seem familiar.

The Rockets went an entire regular season without a general manager. Still, Houston won a championship sans a traditional basketball operations executive—perhaps a first in NBA history.

The Rockets' starting small forward was traded and untraded. Still, Houston won a championship.

The Rockets started 22–1, yet were not in first place on April 1. Still, Houston won a championship.

The Rockets lost the first two games of the Phoenix playoff series at home. Still, Houston won a championship.

The Rockets trailed New York 3–2 in the NBA Finals. Still, Houston won a championship.

Coach Rudy Tomjanovich says it has been his experience that the best things in life never come easily. You have to have known the lowest lows to appreciate the highest highs.

Through the good days and the bad, this team—individually and collectively—never surrendered. It is a team of character, not characters. And that is why the Rockets have carved an everlasting niche in Houston sports history.

An NBA season is like a long-running mystery. There are clues along the way that give you an idea about what might transpire during the final scene. It is important to know what happened in the beginning and in the middle to fully appreciate what happened to a team and its city in the end.

Follow the Rockets on the airplane, through the hotel, in the locker room and on the court. Share the light moments and the heavy moments. This is the day-to-day story of a team that dodged a lot of potential nightmares and wound up in Dreamland, boosting the spirit of Houston's long-suffering sports fans in the process.

Special thanks to B.J. Lowe of Gulf Publishing and Gerald Garcia, Ernie Williamson, Steven Jeffress, Jim Preston and Mike Read of *The Houston Post* for their help in making this project a reality.

For me, writing this book has been a labor of love. This is the way it happened in the unforgettable season of '93–'94.

Enjoy the journal.

And enjoy the journey.

Robert Falkoff

CHAPTER ONE

Preseason: The Dream Begins

August 30, 1993

As usual, I was in the wrong place at the wrong time. There's nothing quite as disconcerting as walking in on the firing squad.

That's how it all started for me as I began compiling a journal of the 1993–94 Houston Rockets season. An inauspicious beginning it was, with cymbals crashing instead of trumpets blaring. I'd heard of drive-by shootings, but this was a drive-by termination notice, shockingly served up by new owner Leslie Alexander to Steve Patterson, the runner-up in last season's Executive of the Year balloting.

I had been on vacation through July and August, the benefit of working a lot of six- and seven-day weeks during the prior Rockets' season. Some people go into "Detox"; I go into "De-Rocks." But now I was getting itchy for some hoops conversation, even though training camp was roughly five weeks away.

On this sultry, summer morning, I decided to drive down to Rockets' headquarters and visit with Patterson, who always welcomed me into his office in an affable manner, whether it meant instant publicity for the Rockets or not.

We talked about whether the club would go after a veteran back-up center prior to camp. We talked about the status of guard Dave

1

Jamerson, who appeared to be on the bubble despite having a year left on his contract.

In general, Patterson felt great about his team, which had come down the stretch 41–11 in '92–'93 before barely dropping a Western Conference semifinal playoff series to Seattle when Vernon Maxwell's last-second, make-or-break shot in overtime of Game 7 fell off the rim.

He was not quite as optimistic when I asked him about the new owner.

"How's it going with the new guy?"

Patterson rolled his eyes skyward and leaned back in his chair.

"It's a learning process," he said.

I didn't read much into that statement. After all, Steve's father—Ray Patterson—had broken in a number of new owners while building the Rockets' franchise in the 1970s. Alexander would probably sit back and evaluate the organization for a year before making any key decisions.

Or would he?

I shook hands with Patterson and left the general manager's office. For 20 minutes, I was across the hall visiting with other Rockets' employees, then headed back into the main hallway which would lead me to the parking lot. There, I ran smack into Alexander, whom I had met only briefly during his early-summer purchase of the club.

Alexander asked me if I wanted to chat a bit. He led me straight into Patterson's office and took a seat behind Patterson's desk. Odd.

Twenty minutes earlier, I had noticed Patterson's sweater draped across an adjacent chair. Now, it was gone. It didn't take Dick Tracy to figure out something very strange was going on here.

After a few minutes of small talk, Alexander—a native New Yorker with a staccato-speaking cadence—confirmed my growing suspicions.

"Wanna know something? I let Steve go today."

Now you see him, now you don't.

Right after I had walked out of Patterson's office, Alexander had walked in and fired him. My first thought was of head coach Rudy Tomjanovich. Patterson and Tomjanovich were tight. They had developed a harmonious working relationship. Rudy wouldn't like this.

"Has Rudy been told?" I asked Alexander.

"Excuse me, I need to do that."

Alexander picked up the telephone and called his secretary. "Get me Rudy on the phone."

A few seconds later, Tomjanovich called back.

"Rudy, I know you liked Steve, but he had to go . . ."

Only when Tomjanovich began his reply did Alexander cup the phone and politely ask me to leave the office.

It had been quite a morning. It's not every day that an owner fires a general manager and informs a sportswriter about it before he gets around to telling his own coach.

Later, as the press descended on The Summit like so many vultures, Alexander said Patterson—who had run both the business and basketball operations—was fired because the business side wasn't up to par. Sure enough, a golf metaphor was appropriate here. Tod Leiweke would be leaving his executive job with the Professional Golf Association, ostensibly to improve the team's bottom line as the club president.

Fine. But why not allow Patterson to continue working with Tomjanovich in basketball operations? Patterson was regarded around the league as a hard-working, bright, energetic man with expert knowledge of the NBA's intricate salary cap. When Tomjanovich wanted to fill a specific personnel need on the club, Patterson always had a firm handle on what could or couldn't be done.

The basketball system wasn't broke, so why mess with it now?

For the short term, there was a saving grace. The '93–'94 roster was basically set, since Patterson's last acts as general manager had been trading for Mario Elie and signing rookie first-round pick Sam Cassell.

But as this season unfolds over the next seven to nine months, you can bet there's going to be a glaring need for a general manager.

Wonder if "Wild, Wild Les" (that's a fitting moniker given to Alexander by *Houston Post* columnist Ray Buck) fully understands that?

Oh, well. I'm going back on vacation.

Why am I suddenly getting the distinct feeling that this Rockets' season is going to be one hell of a wild ride?

My television is tuned to the Toronto Blue Jays versus the Chicago White Sox in Game 1 of the American League Championship Series. My wife Jackie and our children, Joey and Laurie, have already gone to bed and I'm dozing in and out on the living room sofa.

Sometimes, you can be asleep and still hear something which causes you to question if it's a dream or reality. I'm sleeping, but I hear sportscaster Greg Gumbel say there is a rumor spreading through Comiskey Park that Michael Jordan is going to retire. Or at least I *think* I hear Gumbel say that.

My eyes open. Now, I'm wide awake. Yeah, Gumbel is saying what I thought he said. There are media reports circulating in Chicago that the world's greatest basketball player will hang up his Air Jordan sneakers at the apex of a wondrous career.

Suddenly, I'm jarred by the ringing of the telephone. The sports department of *The Houston Post* is calling. The Jordan bombshell is now on the Associated Press wire, and the office wants me to call somebody from the Rockets for a quick reaction.

I call the Tomjanovich residence, and Sophie Tomjanovich, the friendly, vivacious wife of the head coach, answers on the second ring.

"Sophie, it's Robert Falkoff. Have you heard the big news?"

"No, we just got home."

"There are reports that Michael Jordan is retiring."

"What? You're kidding. Wait a minute, here's Rudy."

I told Tomjanovich the bits and pieces of information that were filtering in. Tomjanovich sounded surprised, but not completely flabbergasted.

"Nobody can imagine what Michael Jordan goes through," Tomjanovich said. "I'm sure he has taken his time and given this a lot of thought."

I asked Tomjanovich what Jordan departure would mean in the big picture. With training camp commencing in three days, most people were picking the Bulls to win a fourth consecutive title. No Jordan, said Tomjanovich, would mean a wide-open race for the championship rings.

"With no Jordan, it changes everything," Tomjanovich said. "The whole NBA picture will be different with the main man not there."

As I hang up the phone, I'm wondering who will be the 1994 world champions. I know Chicago can't get there without Jordan. New York will be the favorite now. Phoenix will be right there if Charles Barkley's back is OK. Seattle will be tough again. And how about the Rockets?

Houston was as good as anybody at the end of last season. Hakeem Olajuwon may now rank as the No. 1 player in the league with Jordan gone, and the Dream is going to be on a mission after the near-miss in Seattle.

The thought flashes through my mind: Houston Rockets, 1994 World Champions.

But quickly, I dismiss this silly fantasy and head off to bed. This is Houston. Everybody knows Houston can't win a pro sports championship.

October 7

It's here. Rockets' Media Day.

This is the official liftoff of the season, with players reporting for physicals, team photographs and interviews. There's never any question about which player the press gravitates toward after a cold-cut lunch. Olajuwon is the man when it comes to delivering the opening-day "State of the Rockets" message.

I figure this year's version won't be nearly as exciting as last year's opening fireworks. That was when Olajuwon was embroiled in a controversy with former owner Charlie Thomas.

"Charlie has been a coward," Olajuwon said on opening day of the '92–'93 season.

Ouch.

The laid-back Thomas, standing only a few feet away, took that verbal haymaker in stride.

"My wife Kittsie has called me worse," Thomas drawled, "and we're still married."

Thomas and Olajuwon eventually patched up their differences, and Olajuwon went on to have a tremendous year, finishing second to Barkley in the MVP balloting. When the Rockets' season ended with the gut-wrencher in Seattle, Olajuwon truly believed in the team and the organization again. He left the Seattle Center Coliseum locker room that day saying "we go from here."

Now, the '93–'94 season was upon him, and Olajuwon would sound the rallying cry.

"Is it realistic to think the Rockets could win a championship?" someone asked.

"It's realistic," Olajuwon said. "We just have to establish our goals earlier. Last year, we didn't have a direction early. But now, we know we're supposed to win. Everybody is so confident to meet the competition. The chemistry is there."

On Media Day, hope springs eternal. Players all across the league talk whimsically about playing until June and winning a title. But who really wants to pay the price of champions during this marathon competition? Who wants to make the extra effort on defense and sacrifice their scoring average and/or playing time for the good of the team? Who can take the media heat with a cool resolve? Who can be humbled by the greatest basketball competition in the world and come back to fight on another day?

We'll begin to start formulating some answers when practice commences tomorrow.

October 8

One week.

That's all the time Tomjanovich and his staff have to lay the foundation for success. A lot of fans think two-a-day training camp sessions in the NBA don't mean much. After all, the *real* competition—the playoffs—doesn't come for seven months.

But coaches will tell you this first week is essential in establishing a philosophy, a commitment and a style that will hold up through good times and bad. Once the preseason games begin, an NBA team is like a traveling circus. You hop from town to town, leaving precious little time for teaching and practice sessions.

With all of this in mind, Tomjanovich shrewdly made the decision before the '92–'93 season to take the Rockets to Galveston for the crucial first week. Here, the players have nothing on their minds except basketball, Mario's pizza, reflective walks on the Seawall and more basketball.

I survey the cast after the preseason's opening practice at Galveston Ball High School and see the old and the new. There's Olajuwon, who already looks in midseason form. There is power forward

Otis Thorpe, hoping to bounce back strong from an injury-marred '92–'93 season. There's high-flying Robert Horry and the starting guards, Maxwell and Kenny Smith.

Scott Brooks, Matt Bullard and Carl Herrera are off and running and newcomers Elie and Cassell look as though they're comfortable in their new surroundings.

I wanted to meet the key newcomers after practice and Cassell was first. I kidded him about having to guard celebrated rookie Anfernee Hardaway in the upcoming preseason opener at The Summit. Hardaway had just signed a whopping $65 million contract.

Cassell thought about that prospect for a moment.

"Hey, he's got to guard me, too," Cassell responded.

Cassell had made a good first impression. I like that attitude.

October 12

On the day he officially took over the team in midsummer, Alexander told the media the Rockets were on the verge of making a "significant" trade. A couple of days later, Elie was acquired from Portland for a second-round draft choice.

Significant? Everybody laughed.

But as I watched Elie flick those three-point set shots after practice today, I had the feeling Les Alexander might have stumbled upon the right adjective.

Around the league, the pundits are saying the Rockets stood pat while clubs such as San Antonio, Phoenix, Utah and Golden State improved dramatically. The Spurs had traded Sean Elliott for Dennis Rodman. Phoenix had signed free agent A.C. Green. Utah was bolstering its bench with Tom Chambers. And the Warriors were adding prize rookie Chris Webber to their stable of perimeter threats.

I knew this much: Tomjanovich felt the unheralded Elie would be a perfect fit on this Rockets' club because he could back up either Maxwell at shooting guard or Horry at small forward.

Tomjanovich had told me Elie was a solid citizen, a warrior, a guy who would drive in key situations or can the big three-pointer. And the contemporary history books had shown Tomjanovich was seldom wrong when evaluating personnel.

I talked to Elie today. He had a certain maturity about him. It was obvious even in casual conversation he knew the game and what he wanted out of it.

"I feel like I'm the right man in the right place," Elie said. "Take my strengths and put them with this team . . . it's a nice match."

The Rockets got Elie because they acted smartly and expeditiously as an organization. Aware that Portland was in a salary-cap bind while trying to sign center Chris Dudley, Houston established contact with the Blazers and positioned itself for an early Christmas present. In order to sign Dudley, the Blazers had to trim Elie's salary from their payroll.

A blockbuster trade? No. A significant trade? Yes.

This guy should help.

October 15

The preseason opener was played tonight with Hardaway, Shaquille O'Neal and the Orlando Magic showing up at The Summit to claim a 95–87 victory. But as it turned out, the game seemed totally insignificant. Tragedy had struck a member of the Rockets' family. Maxwell's wife, Shell, had delivered a stillborn child—Amber—and the team had spent part of the day at the highly emotional funeral.

Maxwell played in the game, hitting 2 of 12 shots. Afterward, I offered my condolences.

"Right now, I'd rather not have anything about it in the newspaper, OK?" Maxwell said softly.

"OK."

It was a grim reminder that beyond this magical world—beyond the seven-figure salaries and the opportunity to play a child's game for a living—there are real people with real heartaches.

Sometimes, we have a tendency to forget that.

October 16

It didn't take long for the commercial versus charter issue to come up. The Rockets are one of the few remaining NBA teams that hasn't gone exclusively to charter airline travel. This morning, they flew from Houston to Atlanta, sat around the airport for awhile and then boarded another plane that would take them from Atlanta to Charleston, S.C., for tonight's game against the Knicks.

The team didn't get to its hotel until around 3:30 p.m. A two-hour rest, and it was time to head to the arena.

This travel regimen may be all right for the traveling salesman. But for a professional basketball team, it's the equivalent of turning the players into a flock of sacrificial lambs. The alternative would have been chartering out of Houston after the Orlando game, sleeping late in Charleston and playing with a tank of energy.

Predictably, the strong-legged Knicks won 106–88.

The Rockets won, too, from a financial standpoint. They saved a bundle of cash by not chartering.

Nobody's griping much now. But if this airline trend continues, rest assured the employer will hear from the employees.

October 17

As bad as the trip to South Carolina was, the return trip home was even worse. Due to mechanical difficulties, the Rockets had to fly from Charleston to Atlanta to Dallas to Houston. They touched down at Intercontinental Airport more than nine hours after their wake-up call. Hardly a nice way to spend an autumn Sunday.

Just call it the lost weekend.

Preseason had started with an 0–2 whimper, not a bang. And the first road trip had been a useless Lost in Space odyssey.

Tomjanovich, however, wasn't particularly worried. He felt the opening loss was partially a result of the team's anguish over the Maxwell situation. The New York score had to be dismissed as any kind of early barometer because of the travel complications.

"I really think it will be another week before we know where we are as a team," Tomjanovich said. "I'm anxious because coaches want to win every game. But you have to be patient. The slow start has gotten our attention. But it's not something to overreact to."

October 24

Rudy was right. Those first two games were an aberration. In the last week, having had the opportunity to get into a normal practice routine at home, the Rockets whizzed past Detroit 125–100 and Dallas 92–83.

Time for a Mexican Fiesta. Tonight is South of the Border night.

For the second year in a row, the Rockets have taken their act to Mexico City. The Houston organization is excited about turning this sprawling metropolis of 23 million into prime Rockets' country, and tonight's game against the Knicks at Palacio de los Deportes will be watched by a sellout crowd of 20,000.

Basic geography aside, it still seems weird that the Rockets can fly two hours and play in a foreign country. Other than San Antonio and Dallas, it's their shortest trip of the year.

Commissioner David Stern has talked about placing an expansion team in Mexico City by the end of the decade. Until then, the Rockets will be Mexico's main NBA ambassadors, and the players don't seem to mind.

"We sure had a easier time getting to Mexico than we did South Carolina," Smith mused.

The Knicks would prevail in a hard-fought game, but the Mexican fans barely noticed the final score. They were intrigued by the *clavadazos* (slam dunks) of Olajuwon and Patrick Ewing, and their approval came in the form of shrill whistles.

Yes, Mexico is Rockets' country. The fans left with smiles on their faces. They were content enough to repeat the NBA's favorite marketing slogan:

Me encanta este juego.

"I love this game."

October 26

Think Olajuwon isn't pumped up for this season?

Tonight at Orlando Arena, he showed that the Rockets' first option is still the golden option. With Houston trailing the Magic 100–99 and down to a do-or-die possession, the Rockets had their first real opportunity of the preseason to practice in a pressure situation.

The ball came to Olajuwon, who turned to the left baseline and sank a game-winner with 3.1 seconds remaining. A preview of coming attractions, perhaps?

With Jordan gone, Olajuwon's shake-and-bake jumper might be the most reliable weapon in the game. Of course, Olajuwon's task would have been more difficult if O'Neal had been defending against him instead of Greg Kite. O'Neal had a slightly sprained ankle, and the Magic wanted him healthy for an upcoming trip to London.

"We executed down the stretch, and it's good to get in a habit of doing that," Olajuwon said. "We're going to be in that situation many times this year. One possession, win or lose, on the road. You've got to be able to finish."

As long as the Rockets have No. 34 to take the big shot, being able to finish shouldn't be a problem.

October 28

In six weeks on the job as the new Rockets' club president, Leiweke has hit the ground running. As much as Tomjanovich and his basketball staff liked Patterson, I thought the transition to dealing with Leiweke would be an awkward proposition.

But the new man is energetic and personable, and he's winning a lot of friends while trying to smooth over the rough feelings created by the dismissal of Patterson and several front-office people from the previous regime.

Over lunch, Leiweke is telling me his visions for the Rockets' franchise, which has had steadily declining attendance since playing to 100 percent capacity in 1988.

"My feeling is that the Houston Rockets have the potential to be a premier franchise in the NBA," he said. "From the fans' perspective, that's based on what happens on the court. But the reality is that what happens on my side of the business will ultimately affect what's going to happen on the court. That's where I come in. I've got to make this a premier business."

Leiweke had been hired virtually on the spot by Alexander at the suggestion of NBA broadcasting executive John Kosner. While working for Golden State in the late 1980s, Leiweke had spearheaded a marketing approach in which the Warriors' season-ticket base went from 1,600 to 13,000—with a waiting list of thousands more.

Indeed, he appeared to have the credentials of a coat-and-tie MVP. Besides working to boost sales through his basic philosophy of making season-ticket holders feel a part of the program, Leiweke said he was intensifying the search for a traditional general manager to fill the basketball void left by Patterson.

"There have been a lot of questions about new ownership, as you would expect," Leiweke said, finishing his dessert. "But I've spent a lot of quality time with Les, and I really believe he wants to do the right thing in the community. I'm satisfied that at the end of the day, Les will be perceived as a really positive thing for the Rockets."

October 31

With the regular season starting Friday night, it's time for those Halloween predictions. I've rubbed off my crystal ball and listed my picks in today's *Post* special section.

New York, Cleveland, Houston and Seattle are my division winners. I've got the Knicks over Cleveland in the Eastern Conference Finals; Phoenix over Houston in the Western Conference Finals and New York over Phoenix in the championship series.

If I'm semi-right, I'll remind everybody.

If not . . . well, nobody will remember in June anyway.

November 1

The preseason schedule ends tonight in Fort Worth. We're staying at the Hyatt Regency at DFW Airport, and I've gone down to the coffee shop for a late lunch/early dinner. Around 5 p.m., Jamerson walks in.

"How you seen Ray Melchiorre (the trainer)?"

"No," I answered. "Are you going to the arena early?"

"I'm going back to Houston," Jamerson replied. "I've been waived."

Everybody knew this was coming. But it was still jarring to hear the words. I really liked and admired Jamerson, a deeply religious young man who had never really received a legitimate chance in his three years with the Rockets since becoming the team's No. 1 draft pick out of Ohio University.

After two apprentice years, Jamerson was about to get his shot at the beginning of the '92–'93 season. But a few days before training camp, he blew out his knee in an informal workout and wound up missing the season.

Jamerson still has a guaranteed year left on his contract. But the terms stipulated that Jamerson would be entitled to the entire $1 million if he were on the opening-night roster. Otherwise, the club could dole out the $1 million in increments over an eight-year period.

With five guards—Maxwell, Smith, Elie, Brooks and Cassell—ranking ahead of Jamerson, the organization wasn't about to overlook the financial loophole in Jamerson's deal.

"It's part of life," Jamerson said. "It just didn't happen for me with the Rockets, but I don't feel any bitterness toward the organization. I think Rudy has been fair and honest."

After Jamerson left the hotel, players began to filter into the lobby. The news spread quickly as the team digested the only significant move of training camp.

"Better him than me," one player muttered.

That sounds cold, but it is like that in professional sports. This is a business of survival. You make your money and, along the way, you make some casual friends.

But you never get too close to the guy at the next locker. He could be out of your life at a moment's notice.

Just as Jamerson was.

CHAPTER TWO

White Hot: November–December

November 3, 1993

Hakeem agreed to sit and talk with me after practice today.

We did the interview on the court, in a darkened and deserted Summit. I came away feeling the main man is truly on a championship mission.

"It's not just rolling the dice," he said. "You can go to any team right now, and they'll say they want to win a championship. But who is really willing to sacrifice? Who is willing to show the work ethic, and who does the smart things?

"It's a day-to-day, unwavering commitment. Maybe you're sincere, maybe the guy at another position is sincere. But it takes a whole team being sincere or it won't happen. It takes hard work, togetherness, unity as one."

I asked Olajuwon if the Rockets have the ingredients he had just described.

"It depends on how much we learned last year," he said. "Realism is knowing you have a good chance, but understanding how hard you have to work and how smart you have to be. We cannot live off last year. We have a good chance if everybody wants it badly enough. But we have to start with that attitude from day one.

"As the year goes on, we will be tested in so many areas. If you lose a game you're supposed to win, you can't fall apart. If the calls don't go in your favor, you can't fall apart. If the press is giving credit only to the high scorers and someone feels his role isn't

14

appreciated, the team has to make sure that player feels appreciated within the family for sacrificing individual goals for team goals.

"We have to reward each other on the court. If I cover for a guard and block his man's shot, maybe he rewards me by getting me a dunk on the other end. That's team basketball.

"The guys who don't play? They have to work their man in practice and get him ready. They are very important, too.

"And the fans . . . we need them. If we're down five or six points, they can't be booing us. They must believe. It takes all of these things to win a championship."

Hakeem said it all. Those are words for the Rockets to live by these next eight months.

November 4

Someone dutifully brought a copy of the *San Antonio Express-News* to practice today. The lead story in the sports section quotes former Rockets' guard Sleepy Floyd as saying his new Spurs' team will "definitely" win the Midwest Division.

Not to be outdone by his longtime buddy, Maxwell looked at the story and decided to go one-up on Floyd.

"We're going all the way," Maxwell decided.

All the way? As in world championship? Any doubts?

"No doubts," Maxwell insisted.

Then, with a laugh, Maxwell added: "Hey, if Sleepy can say it, I can, too."

Typical "Mad Max." Even in the prediction business, he's a competitor.

The other news of the day wasn't so lighthearted.

Neal Talmadge, the club's former director of corporate sales who was ousted in the Alexander takeover, has announced through his lawyer he is suing the organization and Alexander for "fraud and/or racial discrimination."

The bitterness between the past and present front-office types seems to get more intense with each passing hour.

November 5

OK, time to get down to serious business.

The curtain went up on the regular season tonight and the premiere was an unqualified success. Houston blew away New Jersey 110–88 at The Summit, with Horry joining Olajuwon in the winner's spotlight.

Horry had suffered through a tenuous preseason, largely because of the acute pain caused by tendinitis in his right knee. But when Horry was put in a situation where the game meant something, adrenaline got the best of tendinitis. Horry hit 7 of 12 shots and added seven rebounds, three steals and a blocked shot.

"From preseason to regular season, it was like night and day," Horry said. "I was so pumped up I just forgot about whether there was pain in my knee. I was so hyped."

So far, so good.

Only 81 more to go.

November 6

Rudy T is no fool. In the aftermath of the Patterson firing, it only made sense that he should push for security and stability for himself and, residually, his loyal basketball staff. In recent weeks, plans have been in the works for a Tomjanovich contract extension—with Leiweke serving as the point man in negotiations with Tomjanovich's Michigan agent.

Word is, the deal could be announced soon. According to Leiweke, the Tomjanovich matter will affect what type of individual the club will go after to head basketball operations.

With Tomjanovich aboard for the long haul, the Rockets would want more of a low-key, nuts-and-bolts man. If the Tomjanovich negotiations were to fall apart, leaving Tomjanovich dangling with only an option year left on his deal, the team might be more inclined to go for more of a high-profile name such as Del Harris.

I ran into Rudy tonight as he was having a late-night snack at the Portland Marriott.

He wasn't at liberty to talk about the contract extension issue but indicated a deal could be imminent.

Then the conversation turned to the 1–0 Rockets. After tomorrow's game against the Blazers, I suggested, the upcoming schedule didn't seem imposing. There were a siege of weak teams and injury-wrecked teams on the horizon.

"If you win this one," I said, "you might be 10–0 going to Utah on Nov. 24."

Tomjanovich waved off that suggestion.

"You know this business," he said, laughing. "It's the old cliche. One at a time. If you overlook any team in the NBA, that's when you get your butt kicked."

November 7

I know the season is really under way now. Mad Max had his first temper tantrum of the year while playing against the Blazers.

It happened in the third quarter when Maxwell was called for his fourth foul against a driving Clyde Drexler.

Quite a show for this early in the season.

Maxwell picked up a double technical and an automatic ejection. Before leaving the Memorial Coliseum floor, he threw a warmup suit and a towel on the court and stopped to engage in conversation with a fan. First-year assistant coach Larry Smith—who's about the only guy around who can handle Maxwell when the big guard loses his cool—had to direct Maxwell to the locker room while Drexler completed a five-point play to tie the game.

"After the first technical, the ref (Luis Grillo) said 'you got anything else to say?' Then he cursed me," Maxwell said. "I spit on the floor."

Luckily for Houston, Elie came along to win one for the spitter.

The ex-Blazer hit a clutch three-pointer to stop Portland's momentum, and the Rockets went on to a 14-point victory.

Hmmm, 2–0. Golden State is next, and that's a team ravaged by injuries. This bolt out of the blocks could get real interesting.

November 9

The more you're around this league, the more you understand how the professional lives of the coaches hinge largely on fate.

As I watch the Rockets beat the heck out of Golden State, I'm struck by the contrast of fate involving Rudy T and Don Nelson. The Warriors' coach thought he had a title contender after drafting Chris Webber. But Chris Mullin is out of the lineup for six weeks and Tim Hardaway and Sarunas Marciulionis are out for the year with knee injuries.

Nelson looks pale and tired. It's the third game of the year, and he already knows he has no shot at true glory. All because of fate.

Here's a man who has long been regarded as a top-notch coach but has never taken a team beyond the conference finals. How deflating this must be for him.

And then there's Rudy.

His team is healthy, athletic and definitely on the rise. The players are working hard for him and tomorrow he'll go home and sign a contract that will give him security through the '98–'99 season.

In this game, you have to be good to stay around and have a shot at the big prize.

You also have to be lucky.

November 10

Les Alexander has put his money where his mouth is.

The news conference to announce Tomjanovich's contract extension was held today after the Rockets flew home from their undefeated West Coast trip. This was good publicity for Alexander, who had been developing a reputation among his ever-changing front-office staff for being more than a little frugal.

"There aren't many great NBA coaches," Alexander said. "He (Tomjanovich) is one of them, and you have to recognize an asset like that. Our players are terrific. They are great kids; they play hard and don't give an inch. But the coach is so important. I think if there was the wrong coach on this team, it would be a .500 team."

No argument there.

November 13

A funny thing happened while the Rockets were in the process of whipping Phoenix for victory No. 5. Late in the game, with Houston up by eight and Charles Barkley headed downcourt, a woman came out of the stands and gave Sir Charles a smooch.

You never know when a Morganna wannabe will strike.

After the game, Smith said the woman should have bypassed Barkley for Olajuwon. Why not kiss this year's MVP, not last year's MVP?

"She kissed the wrong guy," Smith said. "This is going to be Hakeem Olajuwon's year."

So far, it is.

But Barkley didn't seem that impressed with the Rockets.

"You shouldn't make a big deal out of anything in November," he said. "Houston is a very good team, one of the top four in our conference. But we're the best team in the world."

We'll see about that, Charlie. We'll see.

November 15

This Rockets' team is fast becoming destiny's darlings. It's a different hero each time out, and tonight the spotlight at Philadelphia's Spectrum belonged to Bullard, the 6–10 free spirit with the velvet shooting touch.

Bullard's preseason had been a disaster because of two freak injuries. In the exhibition opener, he was inadvertently poked in the eye, which forced him to miss valuable practice time. He came back in Mexico City, only to suffer a sprained ankle.

So, it was really no surprise when a rusty Bullard opened the season shooting 2 of 17 from the floor through five games. Tonight, however, he bailed the Rockets out of a 12-point hole in the fourth quarter by scoring 11 points down the stretch, including three treys.

Bullard has a variety of interests in life. He loves to go bass fishing, jam on the drums, tee up the golf ball, listen to music and catch a few rays by the pool. But what he does best is launch that three-pointer with perfect backspin.

It's interesting to watch the dynamics of a team on a roll. The pieces fit like a complex jigsaw puzzle.

The Rockets had received virtually nothing from Bullard before tonight. But with the undefeated record on the line and the team struggling through three quarters, they needed that extra boost from an X-factor.

Everybody's pulling their weight now.

Will this team ever lose?

Same song, eighth verse.

The Rockets completed a sweep of their three-game Eastern road trip tonight with a victory over Indiana. Houston is 8–0 for the second time in club history and—in the cramped dressing-room quarters at Market Square Arena, Olajuwon is wondering what type of reception the Rockets' fans will provide when Houston gets home.

So far, home attendance has been lukewarm, to put it kindly. The big sports news in Houston continues to be the Oilers and the Astros' signing of new manager Terry Collins. The Rockets? It seems they're doing all this good work in a vacuum.

"Maybe our fans are from Missouri—they have to be shown," Olajuwon said. "Well, we're 8–0. We've gone out and shown them.

"We've been to a lot of cities where they're dying to have a franchise. Their teams aren't winning, but they fill the stadium for every game."

If the 8–0 record doesn't impress Rockets' fans, the defensive statistics certainly should. It is becoming increasingly clear this team has picked up defensively where it left off last year in a closing 41–11 regular-season run.

On this road trip, Houston's fourth-quarter defense allowed 11, 13 and 14 points.

"That's just tightening the screws," Tomjanovich marveled.

One more for the club-record winning streak to start a season.

But will the sports fans in Houston really notice?

Never has it been so easy to float atop Cloud Nine.

The Rockets had no problem blasting by the woeful Clippers for No. 9 in a row. Yes, nine is the magic number. Tomjanovich is working with a nine-man rotation—with Bullard, Herrera, Brooks and Elie giving Houston a solid if not spectacular bench.

Still, there are some skeptics out there. Houston's nine opponents have a combined record of 24–39. All-Star Danny Manning didn't play tonight, and scorer deluxe Reggie Miller didn't play in the previous game for Indiana.

Tomjanovich shrugged off the weak-schedule theory.

"I think that's kind of overblown," he said. "We have to be up every night because we're a hot item in the league right now. We're going to get everybody's best game."

November 23

What a downer. The three-time defending champion Chicago Bulls have come to Houston without Mr. Jordan.

That's like going to Magic Kingdom and not seeing Mickey Mouse.

The reality of Jordan's departure didn't really hit me until I saw the Bulls trot out for their pregame warmups. Suddenly, this was just another team with no more pizazz than an Indiana or a Milwaukee.

To make it even worse, guys such as Scottie Pippen, Bill Cartwright, Scott Williams and John Paxson weren't there, either. Basically, the Rockets had to beat the Bulls' junior varsity to go to 10–0.

This game marked the true coming-out party of Cassell, who was starting in place of the injured Smith.

The rookie struggled early with 1 of 7 shooting and four turnovers. He'll start again tomorrow in Utah, which is where I figure the Rockets will finally introduce themselves to a loss.

It has been a nice run. But hey, nobody wins them all.

November 24

Oops. Scratch yesterday's prognostication.

The Rockets are truly making this a November to remember. Down by two with five seconds remaining in regulation, they found a way to tie the game and then win in overtime. Elie was the definitive hero. He made a bold drive and drew a foul, then hit two pressure free throws with 2.1 seconds remaining.

After that Super Mario moment, no way the Rockets were going to allow their streak to be snapped.

It was a great present on Tomjanovich's 45th birthday.

"I couldn't be prouder of this group of guys," Tomjanovich shouted. "How 'bout them Rockets?"

This was the first clear sign that Houston's streak was going to be one for the ages. You just don't go into Utah in a back-to-back situation and beat the Jazz unless you've got a lot of strong-minded athletes and a serious will to win.

Cassell got another start at the point, and this time he responded with a major contribution. The rookie finished with 15 points in 23 minutes while going toe-to-toe with All-Pro John Stockton.

The 11–0 Rockets will fly to Sacramento tomorrow, and they'll have Thanksgiving dinner there in a private banquet room at the Hyatt. For a team that hasn't tasted defeat, that turkey should taste great.

"We've got a lot to be thankful for," Tomjanovich said.

Indeed.

November 25

I've got to believe the NBA schedule-maker has some kind of Thanksgiving curse going against the Rockets. In 15 years of covering this team, I can only remember three or four times when the club wasn't stuck on the road for this holiday.

It sure would be nice if we were at home with our families today, watching the Macy's Thanksgiving Day parade on television and smelling that turkey roasting in the oven. This is when the road starts to look very lonely.

But then again, it could be worse.

The Rockets are chartering on the San Antonio Spurs' posh, private plane this trip. They've come a long way since that nauseating, puddle-jumping sojourn to South Carolina last month.

Still, Thorpe found it ironic that the Rockets were using the aircraft of their Interstate 10 rivals.

"We're 11–0," Thorpe said, "and have to use San Antonio's plane."

After the Rockets flew from Salt Lake City to Sacramento, they had a few hours to rest before Thanksgiving dinner. The evening's entertainment was provided by Hall of Famer and television analyst Calvin Murphy, who can be about as funny as Eddie Murphy when he gets on a roll.

Murphy provided his rollicking version of Dallas Cowboy lineman Leon Lett's memorable *faux pas* against the Dolphins earlier in the day. Then Murphy applied the needle to Smith, who was rejoining the team after missing two games with patellar tendinitis in his left knee. Murphy joked that Smith had hurried back after watching Cassell score those 15 points and hit three treys against the Jazz.

"I knew you'd be here," a beaming Murphy ribbed Smith. "I think it was Sam's third three-pointer that did it."

I'm not sure Kenny appreciated the humor.

The only glitch in this 11–0 start is the subtle makings of a quarterback controversy. Tomjanovich is continuing the general pattern established last year. Smith starts at the point and Brooks finishes. In the opening nine games, Smith played only 13 minutes in the final period while Brooks played 89 minutes. Now, Smith sits out a couple of games, and Cassell steps in nicely.

It's simple arithmetic. Tomjanovich has three competent point guards and can only use two. Whatever the coach does with his rotation this year, there's going to be a point guard feeling like the odd man out.

November 27

Last night, the Rockets slopped out another win at Sacramento, thanks to some down-the-stretch heroics by Olajuwon. They took a quickie flight to Los Angeles immediately after the game and fell asleep with a 12–0 record, which equals the third-best start in NBA history.

Undefeated and unrelenting. But the Rockets aren't the only team on fire. The Seattle SuperSonics won last night to move to 10–0. Who's going to blink first?

This topic is on my mind as I walk down a hallway at the Marina del Rey Ritz Carlton and knock on Rockets' radio man Gene Peterson's door. Gene has me on his pregame show before each game and sometimes likes to tape the segment before the team heads to the arena.

I know the Rockets will still be undefeated when the segment airs before the 9:30 (Houston time) game against the Clippers. So I talk about the 12–0 Rockets and 10–0 Sonics.

"Maybe they ought to just send these two undefeated teams to the Orange Bowl and let them settle the No. 1 question right there," I said on the tape.

Back in my room, I happen to glance at the Los Angeles Times. Uh-oh.

The Sonics are playing the Cavs tonight in a 6:30 p.m. (Houston time) game. If the Sonics win, I'm OK. But it's possible Seattle will have its first loss by around 8:45, well before the taped interview goes out on the Rockets' radio network.

I'm beginning to panic as I arrive at the Sports Arena. As bad luck would have it, the Sonics are trailing in the third quarter. I hurriedly explain the situation to Peterson, who graciously agrees to bail me out by redoing the interview. This time, we don't touch on the Seattle situation.

Seattle loses and the Rockets win 82–80 when Olajuwon breaks a tie with his patented turnaround jumper at the 22-second mark.

Like I said, there's only one undefeated team in the NBA.

November 28

Tomjanovich spelled it out for the players on the Sunday morning flight home.

As the aircraft was humming at 35,000 feet, the coach walked toward the back of the plane and stressed the importance of not taking the Milwaukee Bucks lightly Tuesday night. If the 13–0 Rockets could take care of business against the Bucks, they would have an opportunity to tie the '48–'49 Washington Capitols' record for best start in NBA history. Better still, they could do it in historic Madison Square Garden, under the watchful eye of the powerful New York media.

Tomjanovich had been leading a campaign to get the Rockets some national respect. What better way to do it than tie the record in the vicinity of Madison Avenue, where images are made?

But first, Milwaukee.

"A game like Milwaukee worries me more than a game against a team with a top record," Tomjanovich said. "Mike Dunleavy is a good coach, and you know they'll be looking forward to playing us. It would be a real feather in their cap if they were the first team to knock us off."

The only question from a Rockets' personnel standpoint is who will start at point guard. Smith claims he's not only ready to play, but ready to start. Cassell has the been the starter the last four games, and the feisty Brooks is still the closer.

If Tomjanovich opts for Smith, it will mean Cassell goes from starting to not playing. If the coach opts to stay with Cassell and bring Smith off the bench, what happens to Brooks?

That's why coaches get paid big money. Decisions, decisions.

November 30

Logic prevailed.

Smith was back in the starting lineup tonight because Tom-janovich has a fundamental policy that a starter cannot lose his job because of injury.

The approach makes sense, particularly since the Rockets are undefeated. You don't mess with the basic chemistry when there's a goose egg in the loss column. Besides, it's a long, long season. The kid from Florida State will probably have plenty of opportunities to play down the line.

The Rockets started slowly, falling behind 15–3. But Houston's talent and depth eventually wore down the lowly Bucks, meaning Houston had capped an incredible, undefeated opening month.

Olajuwon for Player of the Month? Tomjanovich for Coach of the Month?

The awards would undoubtedly be rolling in soon. And now, the Rockets would indeed have the chance to go for a share of the get-away record in The Big Apple.

"When you're a kid shooting hoops in the driveway, you dream of being in the Garden, playing a game like this," Tomjanovich said. "This is fun. This is what it's all about."

One problem: Elie, who has been so valuable in the 14–0 start, suffered a chipped fracture of the third metacarpal bone in his right hand against the Bucks. Too bad. Elie is a native New Yorker and would kill to play in a game like the one coming up.

For what it's worth, I don't think the Rockets can beat the Knicks at the Garden without him.

December 1

I figure it's about time to hear from some old Celtics regarding the contemporary 14–0 Rockets. Tommy Heinsohn, who played on the '57–'58 Celtics' team which started 14–0, is a Boston broad-caster these days. The Celtics are in Atlanta tonight, so I call Hein-sohn and ask him how the hell an NBA team can go this long with-out a defeat.

"It's a great feat, particularly in this era of free agency, contract hassles and all the other distractions and upheaval that can go on in the off-season," Heinsohn said. "To run up a big win streak at the start of the year, you really have to have your act together. In our (Boston) years, we made very few personnel changes. We had a system, and we were in great condition.

"That gave us a jump on the other teams. It's obvious that Houston has a system and a definite idea about about how to win. Once you know *how* to win, you have the potential to win every game. The Rockets found out how to win last year and came back this year with their act together."

Heinsohn said one factor in Houston's 14–0 start is that most clubs in this league are struggling for an identity.

"There are only about five teams right now that are in sync," he said. "It's to Houston's credit that they have capitalized by coming out of training camp full steam ahead. When you want to take a play to Broadway, you start in New Haven (Conn.) or someplace like that with rehearsals. You get all the character actors and the headliners refining their roles.

"A basketball team is the same way. They go to training camp and work on making everything mesh. The ones that are successful with that mission have the possibility of a big start."

Arnold "Red" Auerbach was the coach of the '48–'49 Washington Capitols' team that started 15–0. It's hard to imagine the legendary Auerbach coaching a team *before* the Celtics. That just puts the significance of this streak in perspective. The Rockets are trying to do something that the acknowledged greatest teams in league history—the '67 Sixers, the '72 Lakers, the '86 Celtics—couldn't do.

"It's harder now to put a winning streak together, but it's also not harder," Auerbach said. "It's harder because there's more parity, but it's not harder because it was harder to win on the road then.

"The officials were different then. Officials have such security in their jobs now, they are tougher on the home teams. In those days, other coaches believed in the players playing their way into shape. But I wanted my players to come in in good shape and then get themselves into top shape."

The Rockets had a brief practice in Houston today, then flew to New York for the big show.

The Knicks are a creditable 9–2 and probably would be undefeated themselves if Patrick Ewing hadn't suffered a neck injury that caused him to miss one game and play at 50 percent efficiency in another. Through a scheduling quirk, New York has been off the last four days, giving those New York tabloids plenty of time to hype this game.

Asked if the Knicks would be downcast should Houston leave the Garden with its streak intact, guard John Starks said, "I don't think that's going to happen. It just won't."

Was that a guarantee?

"I'm not guaranteeing anything," Starks responded. "I'm just saying it won't happen."

Thorpe begged to differ.

"The Knicks have a reputation of playing very physical basketball, and the refs let them get away with it," Thorpe said. "We are the better team. We just have to go out and play our game, and we will get it done."

Frankly, I can't remember an early-season NBA game getting this much attention.

December 2

Football season or not, the Rockets are going to have the city of Houston's full attention after what happened tonight. The Rockets didn't just beat the Knicks; they kicked them all the way to 42nd and Broadway.

I don't know what Pat Riley was thinking about. Maybe he put too much mousse in his hair and it affected his brain. Riley hung Ewing out to dry by having him take Olajuwon 1-on-1. That was the ticket for Olajuwon to score 37 points and firmly establish himself as the front-runner for the Most Valuable Player award.

The Rockets showed Ewing much more respect. They doubled down and forced New York to make the outside shots. Starks was able to come through, but the other Knicks' perimeter threats were ice cold.

Before tip-off, Knicks' forward Anthony Mason had rolled his eyes and scoffed at the notion of the Rockets keeping the streak intact.

"Not in our house," Mason said.

The Rockets huffed and puffed and blew the house down.

"That was a great performance by a great team," Riley said. "With all the pressure of the streak, they came into our building and dominated us."

Houston's defense was in near-perfect rhythm and Carl Herrera— who had been disappointing in the opening 14 games—battled the thick-chested Knicks for 14 rebounds. The guts of the team was best symbolized by Elie, who played 19 minutes with the chipped bone in his shooting hand. He still managed to play tough defense and scored his only basket with the left hand.

"This is the one that will really give us national respect," Elie said.

Tomjanovich delivered a series of bear hugs after this record-tying win. The way he was doling out superlatives, he needed a Roget's Thesaurus.

"These players will tell their grandchildren about this," he said.

Somebody asked Tomjanovich if this victory possibly could have a long-term significance. There's already speculation these two teams might meet in the NBA Finals.

"If we have to come back here and win . . . well, it helps to have already done it," Tomjanovich said.

The 15–0 Rockets go for the record tomorrow night in Atlanta. Would you believe 82–0?

December 3

Sometimes, the biggest challenge isn't winning the game. It's getting TO the game.

The Rockets flew out right after the New York extravaganza. Or at least, they tried to. *Houston Post* columnist Kenny Hand and I arrived in Atlanta today and promptly learned the Rockets' traveling contingent had a very rough night.

I'm getting the impression it was sort of like Jack Lemmon in *The Out-of-Towners,* where every possible travel dilemma snowballs into a hopeless mess.

The team tried to charter out of Newark, N.J., but there was a lengthy delay. Finally, the plane took off and landed in Atlanta.

But alas, there was no bus to take the team to its downtown hotel.

The players didn't drag themselves into their rooms until about 4 a.m., and it showed tonight. Hawks 133, Rockets 111. Olajuwon's Victory Tour Across America was finally over.

Somewhere, Auerbach was probably lighting one of his famous cigars. Auerbach's Capitols were still in the record books, tied with the Rockets for fastest getaway.

"Over the course of 16 games, chances are you'll have a stinko," Tomjanovich said. "We had ours tonight."

It had been a dizzying experience, this 15–0 romp to glory.

The pressure kept building and building over a 29-day span, yet the Rockets refused to yield. Had Houston arrived in Atlanta at a decent hour, I'm not even sure the Hawks would have broken the streak tonight.

Certainly, the Rockets have put themselves in position to have a 60-win season, which is considered the general barometer for a title team. Certainly, the Rockets have received an early lesson in handling pressure.

But what will it all mean in the long run? Will this strong-will experience bring about a major residual benefit next spring?

The '49 Capitols of Auerbach didn't win the championship after their blazing start.

I fall asleep in Atlanta wondering if the Rockets will.

December 4

The office suggested doing a story comparing this year's Rockets to the '86 Rockets, who won the Western Conference championship before falling to Boston in the finals.

That's a good thought. Is this year's team the best in club history?

I'd love to see the '85–'86 Rockets and the '93–'94 Rockets square off in one of those computerized video games. Anyway, the guy to talk to about this was longtime Houston Assistant Coach Carroll Dawson, who has worked with both clubs.

Dawson said it would be great offense versus great defense.

"Our '86 team was better offensively, and this year's team is better defensively," Dawson said. "The chemistry is a little better now, but the '86 team was very talented offensively. It was really hard to keep us from scoring. Back then, we won in a different way."

The '86 Rockets started the season 20–0 at home. Olajuwon, Ralph Sampson and Rodney McCray had tremendous size and speed. John Lucas was a pure point guard, and Lewis Lloyd had open-floor skills which were compared to those of Julius Erving.

The Houston bench included a defensive stopper in Mitchell Wiggins, a blue-collar rebounder in Jim Petersen and an instant-offense threat in Robert Reid.

In terms of work ethic, Dawson told me he would give the edge to the current team.

"I've never been around a team that works as hard as this one," he said.

Still, Dawson noted that the burden of proof is on the 15–1 Rockets.

"The '86 team pretty much did it," he said. "They defeated a great Lakers' team 4–1 and played for the world championship. This year's team is off to a great start, but that's all it is right now. We're trying to work our way where the other team has been."

December 6

Well, the "losing streak" was snapped last night.

The Rockets went to 16–1 overall and an outrageous 10–1 on the road by winning a game in Cleveland that they really had no business winning. Trailing by seven with 2:43 remaining, Olajuwon got busy offensively and defensively, setting the stage for Maxwell to win the game with a right-wing trey at the 31-second mark.

Cleveland led for 47:28 and came away with nothing. The Rockets are inventing ways to win now. This is getting ridiculous.

When the team arrived home this morning at Intercontinental Airport, it was greeted by about 200 fans and the Willowridge High School marching band. The reception was set up by the club to honor the Rockets' NBA record-tying start.

I couldn't recall an airport reception since the Rockets came home from Boston after the '86 Finals. For eight years, this team had filed off airplanes with nobody in its path to baggage claim except the shoeshine man.

And to think it's only early December.

"This kind of thing . . . it can only make the team want to try that much harder," Tomjanovich said as he signed autographs, accepted congratulations and awaited his luggage.

Maybe we'll look back on this scene as the early stages of hero worship.

On most evenings, Thorpe is all meat and potatoes. Tonight, he got the dessert.

From the outset against the Charlotte Hornets, the Houston power forward was enjoying himself to the fullest. Usually, it's Olajuwon who carries the frontline scoring load while Thorpe performs the blue-collar chores in the trenches.

But with Larry Johnson struggling with a bad back and Thorpe having his way with fast-break jams and low-post power moves, Olajuwon deferred to his first lieutenant. Thorpe wound up scoring a career-high 40 points. A 59 percent foul shooter last year, he astounded the Hornets by going 12 of 12 from the line.

That's the thing about these 17–1 Rockets. You never know who's going to jump up with an extrordinary effort. And when it happens, Tomjanovich and the team encourage that individual to bask in the spotlight.

Tomjanovich kept Thorpe in this blowout game late, so Thorpe could get his career high. I don't think Charlotte Coach Allan Bristow minded at all. This wasn't about showing anybody up; it was about giving a deserving individual his due.

Thorpe could average 20 points a game on a different team. He proved that in Sacramento. But with the Rockets, he is asked—on most nights—to sacrifice offensively. This was a chance to reward him, which can only enhance team unity in the long run.

Each night, I'm seeing bits and pieces of a process that can make this basketball team special.

December 9

Miami guard Harold Miner gets the early-season brainlock award.

Here was the situation: The upstart Heat led the Rockets by three points with 3.6 seconds remaining at The Summit. After a timeout, Houston would have the ball in the frontcourt.

Miami Coach Kevin Loughery specifically told Miner to foul Maxwell rather than allow Maxwell to get off a potential tying trey.

But that sound advice goes in Miner's right ear and out the left, allowing Maxwell to pull off yet another Houdini escape.

The Rockets throw the ball to Maxwell, who spins to his left and jacks up a 35-foot prayer. Nothing but net.

After the Maxwell miracle at Ten Greenway Plaza, there's no way the Rockets would let it get away in overtime.

Kudos to Maxwell, but Miner ought to be fined for not doing what Loughery told him. He let down his team, which had played a great game.

"If Miner fouls, we win . . .," Loughery hissed. "All we had to do was foul, and we didn't do it."

The Rockets will take it and not look back.

At the end of the year, the dramatic shot by Maxwell will no doubt be on the club's highlight reel. All's well that ends with the irrepressible Maxwell.

"I can't lie, it was a lucky shot," Maxwell said as he hunched forward and unlaced his sneakers. "But, like Kenny Smith said, if anybody could make that shot, it was me."

Good 'ole Vernon. He can make your cry, or make you laugh.

How much fun are the Rockets having?

Consider the classic prank Bullard played on rookie Eric Riley at the end of the game. Bullard somehow tied Riley's shoelaces together without Riley knowing it. When Riley got up from the bench at the end of the game, he fell forward in a heap with those on the Rockets' bench doubling over with laughter.

Ah, winning. There's nothing like it.

December 10

Today, I put together an advance story on this week's "Game of the Century." Tomorrow at The Summit, the 18–1 Rockets will meet the 16–1 Sonics. Never before in NBA history have two teams gone this late into a season with only one loss each.

We're billing this one as Joe Frazier versus Muhammad Ali; the irresistible force versus the immovable object. It's like the New York game in terms of hype. Even *USA Today* is giving it big play.

I go to the Rockets' practice at Rice University and run into Purvis Short, the former NBA sharpshooter who now works for the Players Association. I got to know Purvis fairly well when he played with the Rockets and I value his basketball insights. So I asked him if he thought the Rockets were an early season flash-in-the-pan or the genuine article.

"It's one of the best teams I've seen in a long time," Short told me. "You often hear about teams fitting the pieces together. The Rockets fit together and that's rare. With all the traveling I'm doing, I see a lot of teams play. I really believe Houston is the best team in basketball right now."

The Sonics, of course, have a different idea.

In terms of scoring differential, they've been much more dominant than Houston to date. Seattle will go into tomorrow's game having outscored its opponents by an astounding average of 14.2 points per outing.

The respective programs of the Rockets and Sonics are almost mirror images in terms of efficiency. Two years ago, within the span of two months, the Sonics hired George Karl as head coach and Houston elevated Tomjanovich. The teams have been soaring in meteoric fashion since.

Karl is an extremely cocky guy, and Tomjanovich is as modest as the day is long. I wouldn't exactly say there's bad blood between the two. But because of their personality differences, I don't think there's much mutual respect there, either.

After the Sonics slipped past the Rockets in overtime of Game 7 in the Western Conference semifinals last year, Tomjanovich congratulated Karl while mentioning the key contribution that reserve guard Dana Barros had made in the second half.

"Yeah, I really pulled a rabbit out of my hat," Karl responded.

Instead of giving Barros the credit, Karl had taken the credit for himself. That's the kind of irritant that could turn Houston-Seattle into a stimulating, juicy rivalry, with two super-competitive coaches right in the spotlight.

December 11

Round I of the Western Conference heavyweight struggle went to the Rockets. The Sonics pride themselves on defense, but were simply beaten at their own game. Houston won 82–75, limiting the Sonics to .316 shooting.

"What a defensive battle," Tomjanovich said. "In the trenches . . . mud all over you. Classic. It reminded me of an old Detroit versus Green Bay football game on Thanksgiving Day."

An appropriate analogy. And the Sonics had the shooting touch of a Packers' offensive lineman.

Afterward, the Sonics weren't throwing any verbal bouquets in Houston's direction. Instead, Karl tried to plant a psychological seed by saying Olajuwon is allowed to play above the rules.

"He has a tremendous grace from the referees," Karl said. "He can play zone, and he can foul."

Olajuwon merely chuckled when told that Karl was saying he gets preferential treatment from the refs.

"I wish he were right," Olajuwon said.

These teams meet again in Seattle in 17 days, and Gary Payton is already vowing that the Rockets will get a whipping.

Another "Game of the Century" to contemplate.

December 13

Time flies when you're on a magic carpet ride.

The 20-game mark is the ceremonial quarter pole in the NBA season. This is when you project everything by multiplying by four.

So, let's see. The Rockets are 19–1. I multiply by four and discover the Rockets will be a spiffy 76–4 through 80 of the 82 games. All they have to do is keep up the current pace.

Well, OK, I'll cut them some slack.

They can ease up a bit and still finish 70–12, which would give them the NBA's all-time best record, breaking the 69–13 mark of the '71–'72 Lakers.

I'm being facetious, of course. Nobody is going to win 70 games in the modern NBA.

But it's fascinating just to play around with such projections because it brings into perspective just how amazing Houston's performance through the opening quarter of the season has been.

A 19–1 record at the quarter pole? I think about it and just shake my head, wondering how this could have happened.

December 14

We're in the Coconut Grove section of Miami, awaiting tonight's game against the Heat, and I'm thinking about . . . Buddy Ryan, of all people.

This guy is generating big news as a defensive coordinator of the Houston Oilers. He even has his own television show. The man is an *assistant* coach, yet he's getting more of the limelight, it seems, than Head Coach Jack Pardee.

By contrast, the Rockets' assistant coaching staff is working in virtual obscurity. The players have been showered with praise and so has Tomjanovich. But what about Dawson, Bill Berry and Larry Smith? Shouldn't they get a sliver of the publicity pie, too?

I decided it was time to do a story on Tomjanovich's bench staff and approached the coach with that premise before the game.

"I'm really glad to talk about that subject, because our staff does so much work and rarely gets recognized," Tomjanovich said. "The assistant coaches are a very, very big part of our success. When they put that 'Rudyball' label on us, it was embarrassing to me. I look at all the help I'm getting. There's a warm, wonderful feeling when you have a family of people who go out there on the same wavelength and have success."

Dawson is a special story. A couple of years ago, he lost vision in one eye. And yet, he sees more through that one eye than most coaches see through two. He is the consummate teacher among the Rockets' assistants, constantly working to upgrade the players' skill level. He is to Tomjanovich what Tex Winter is to Phil Jackson in Chicago.

While the assistants have overlapping duties, Berry—a former coach at San Jose State—is basically a preparations man. He has to condense the scouting reports so that the players can quickly absorb the material they need to know about an upcoming opponent.

Smith joined the staff last summer after a distinguished 13-year pro career. His forte was rebounding, and that's an area in which Houston suffered greatly last year. Smith is a dignified, strong presence with an impeccable work ethic. Having played with several of the current Rockets, he is filling a special niche on the staff.

"There aren't any egos on this staff," Dawson said. "Rudy's a blue-collar guy, and we all have the same mission, which is to help this team become the best it can be. Rudy has set the tone by getting the players to believe in the philosophy. We know as a team what we have to do to win. When players accept the philosophy and the system, that makes coaching very rewarding.''

Tomjanovich will get the bulk of the coaching credit if the Rockets keep up their white-hot pace. But somebody has to tighten the nuts and bolts in this Houston machine. Dawson, Berry and Smith have done that with quiet precision.

Too bad they can't get their own television show, like Buddy Ryan.

December 15

I know it's starting to sound like a broken record, but the 20–1 Rockets won again last night over a tired Miami team. Maxwell, who hails from Gainesville, Fla., always seems to play well in his home state. He scored 16 of his 25 points in the fourth quarter and then revealed his primary motivation.

Maxwell claimed former Heat personnel man Stu Inman told him before the 1988 draft he wasn't ready for the NBA. The fact that Inman now works for Dallas hasn't prompted Max to lift his grudge against the Heat.

Oh, and there's another reason why Maxwell likes to play in his home state.

"They have hot gyms in Florida," he explained. "I get real loose."

Whatever it takes. On the Continental flight home this morning, the streaking Maxwell looked as comfortable as—well, as a Florida flamingo.

December 17

Christmas is just around the corner, and some of the Rockets' players believe the movers and shakers of the NBA are modern-day Scrooges.

Instead of sitting around their living-room trees and opening gifts with their loved ones on Christmas morning, the Rockets will have to settle for room-service eggnog in Phoenix.

The Rockets have been selected to play the Suns in the NBA's opening telecast on NBC. Thorpe doesn't like the idea of Christmas on the road one bit.

"Christmas is a day for sitting back and enjoying your family," he said. "I could see maybe having a game on Christmas Eve, but not Christmas Day. That's what I feel in my heart.

"At the same time, it's a big day for business in the NBA, and we're part of that business. So, we just have to make adjustments."

The good part is that the Rockets will be allowing team family members to fly to Phoenix. Somebody has to provide the entertainment for the millions of people at home, I guess.

But what about those toddlers whose daddies work for the Rockets?

Will Santa Claus be able to find them at the Ritz Carlton in Phoenix?

December 18

The big issue now is whether the Rockets can set a record for the best one-loss start in league history. They had no problem getting past hapless Dallas tonight, which means they need a win at San Antonio and at home against Denver to equal the '69–'70 New York Knicks' mark of 23–1.

The historical significance is that the '70 Knicks, led by Walt Frazier, Bill Bradley and Willis Reed, went on to win a world championship. If Houston can get to 23–1, the connotation would be that they'd done something of true championship caliber. Remember, the 15–0 Washington Capitols finished as a runner-up.

Getting past the Spurs at the Alamodome will be a major hurdle. They're expecting a crowd in excess of 33,000 for Tuesday's game, and it will be Houston's first look at the David Robinson/Rodman tandem.

Tough.

December 21

Never mind about Rodman.

The bizarre one wasn't allowed to suit up because the NBA fined and suspended him for an altercation with Chicago's Stacey King last week. Nevertheless, the Spurs had control of the game with 2:22 remaining. They led 88–83 when Thorpe was called for a flagrant foul. But J.R. Reid gave Houston hope by missing both free throws, followed by a missed jumper from Willie Anderson.

With a chance to get four points, the Spurs got none. That gave the Rockets an opportunity.

One hustle play seemed to symbolize Houston's commitment through 23 games: San Antonio was up three with less than a minute to go. Maxwell missed a trey, but Olajuwon fought for the offensive rebound and kicked it outside. Elie measured a trey, but it missed. Thorpe split two San Antonio players and, with a tremendous effort, tapped the ball not once but twice to set up Maxwell.

This time, the three-pointer went in with 26 seconds remaining. San Antonio broadcaster Dave Barnett summed up the supreme offensive rebounding sequence by saying: "That's just refusing to lose."

That's what it was, all right. The Rockets refusing to lose.

Houston got the ball back for the last shot, and Maxwell got the call. He veered right on the dribble and fired an off-balance jumper just before the clock flashed zero. Swish.

The 22–1 Rockets stormed the court and mobbed Maxwell, looking like a team that had just won the championship.

After the game-winner, Maxwell had more motivation stories. He gets up for the Spurs like he gets up for those Florida teams.

"First of all, San Antonio sold me to Houston for $50,000—like a piece of meat," Maxwell said. "That motivates me. And secondly, I was going up against my good friend John Lucas. He talked to me about an hour on the phone yesterday, telling me what I *wasn't* going to do."

Later, there was an impromptu gathering of Rockets' personnel at Dick's Last Resort on the Riverwalk. ESPN was showing the highlights of the incredible Houston comeback, and Tomjanovich loved seeing the video.

During the short walk back to the hotel, Tomjanovich gazed at the still river, reflected on his team's joyride and uttered a succinct statement that sticks in my mind.

"This," Tomjanovich said, "is a special season."

I'm beginning to believe it.

December 23

Guess who showed up at The Summit tonight? Houstonian George Bush.

His timing wasn't too good, however, because it would have required a presidential pardon to save the suddenly flat Rockets.

Well, so much for equaling the '69–'70 Knicks for best one-loss start.

In something of a shocker, the young Nuggets sped away in the second half to record a 106–93 victory. Denver had come into the game just 2–11 on the road.

"You can't take anything away from Denver," Maxwell said. "They just beat us today. The other game we lost, in Atlanta, I felt it was because we were tired. This is the first time in 24 games that I can accept the loss."

A glance at the schedule would indicate there might be more trouble on the horizon. There's a four-game Christmas road trip coming up which includes stops at Phoenix and Seattle.

If the Rockets fall in Phoenix, they will have lost more games in a three-day span than they lost in the opening 51 days of the season.

To fully measure a team's character, it's important to know how that club will react in rocky times as well as the good times.

Cinderella's slipper disappeared tonight.

Could it be that the real drama is just beginning?

December 24

For this holiday road trip, the Rockets' traveling contingent is much larger than usual. Family members of the standard travelers have been invited, and The Boss is on board, too.

I congratulated Les Alexander on his timely purchase of a 22–2 team.

"If the Rockets win the title, the team's value might go up $25 million," I suggested.

"I think it already has, based on what we've done so far and all the national attention we've received," Alexander responded.

Ho, ho, ho. Merry Christmas.

December 25

It was as though the Rockets all had clauses in their contracts that prohibits them from working on holidays.

The Phoenix Suns steamrolled Houston 111–91 and, from now on, Charles Barkley and Kevin Johnson should be known throughout Houston as the Ghosts of Christmas Past.

Barkley scored 38 points, and . ohnson added 36 as Phoenix shot .524 from the field and provided the Suns' fans who gave up their Christmas afternoon with plenty of holiday cheer.

"We couldn't beat a junior high team if we don't run back on defense, and we didn't run back today," Tomjanovich said. "Barkley and Johnson are great players and will get their points. But instead of scoring in the 20s, they were in the 30s because we didn't run back and make Phoenix play us 5-on-5."

Bah, humbug.

With a chance to show their skills on national television, the Rockets looked nothing like the team that had opened the season 22–1.

"I think it's a normal correction," Olajuwon said, preferring a stock market analogy. "We can't panic because we have lost two in a row. Now, we have to regroup and show mental toughness. We had a fantastic run, and now we've taken a little slip. We just have to get back to playing our game."

December 26

Smith really had a rough time yesterday against K. J. The Phoenix game certainly wasn't all Kenny's fault. But when one starting point guard gets 36 points and the other starting point guard gets four . . . well, you get the picture.

My sense is that Smith has been playing tight because of the three-man logjam at the point. Through 25 games, he has averaged just 9.1 points and 3.5 assists. The statistics haven't mattered because the team has done so well. But if the Rockets are going stay on a smooth course all year, Smith will have to be a big part of the equation.

With that thought in mind, I sought out Smith before tonight's tip-off at The Forum and asked him what's up with his game.

"I've got to open the floor and take some chances," he said. "I've just been making the conservative plays. After the Phoenix game, I decided I was going back to doing the things I know I can do. I've got to be more aggressive and take my game to another level."

"It's going to change tonight," he added with a wink.

Sure enough, Smith torpedoed the Lakers for a career-high 41 points. Tomjanovich rode the hot hand, and Smith hit 16 of 24 shots, including 3 of 6 three-pointers, in Houston's blowout victory.

"That's the Kenny Smith I know," Maxwell said.

Just call it the power of positive thinking.

December 27

A funny message was delivered during a three-hour food revolt on tonight's flight from Los Angeles to Seattle.

Sorry, health nuts. The Rockets are not a team of vegetarians, and nobody is going to turn them into vegetarians.

The players were expecting to have catered meals from Aunt Kizzy's—a Marina del Rey restaurant—on the flight. Didn't happen.

Nanci Alexander, wife of the owner, is a vegetarian, and the players were saying she established the final group menu. She got a vegetarian meal on board and so did everybody else.

Nanci, a very nice lady, ate her food. Most of the players didn't bother picking up a fork.

"Rabbit food," scoffed one player.

After the team arrived at its Seattle hotel, there was a player parade to the meat eateries while Tomjanovich talked to Alexander in the middle of the lobby.

Wonder what that conversation was about?

December 28

The *Seattle Post-Intelligencer* has fanned the flames of controversy while advancing tonight's Rockets-Sonics rematch.

In the Dec. 11 game at The Summit, Horry had been pushed into the Seattle bench by Shawn Kemp. In his haste to get back into the play, Horry toppled Bob Kloppenburg, the 66-year-old Seattle assistant coach.

Kloppenburg had questioned why Horry didn't come into the Sonics' locker room to see if he was OK. Horry responded that Kloppenburg was "senile" for suggesting malice of forethought.

All of that rhetoric—17 days old—was brought to light again as the Rockets awoke to big headlines and a story about the Horry-Kloppenburg affair. The inference was that the Sonics would be motivated tonight as a result of the Horry-Kloppenburg subplot.

"What really boils me is calling a guy senile because he's old," Kloppenburg was quoted as saying. "That's age discrimination, and it's classless."

Horry was heavily booed during the game, but responded with one of his finest outings of the season. It wasn't nearly enough.

The Sonics rattled Houston early with a chaotic trap that forced a siege of turnovers and enabled Seattle to build a 30-point lead. The Rockets settled down and chipped 27 points off the deficit. But then Seattle roared away for a 112–97 victory.

"They wanted it more than we did," Maxwell said. "We got too far behind and used up all our energy making that run. We had some people who weren't ready to play tonight."

The highlight of the evening for Horry was being escorted onto the court by a police officer. Obviously, the Seattle fans had been reading the newspaper and listening to the Horry-bashing on the radio shows.

"That bodyguard made me feel like a rock star," Horry joked.

The fans forgot about Horry as their team poured it on.

So, the Rockets head on to Minnesota for their final game of 1993. At 23–4, they're a game down to Seattle in the loss column for the first time this season.

Maybe it's time to make a few New Year's resolutions.

December 29

Poor Scotty Brooks.

The little guy has felt miserable this trip because of an ill-timed, severe case of the flu. Scotty said he felt it coming on during the last home game against Denver. He was really under the weather on the flight to Phoenix and was so sick Christmas morning there was no way he could play against the Suns.

Couldn't even keep anything down for Christmas dinner, he told me.

Brooks wasn't any better by the time the team got to Los Angeles, but at least he was able to rest in his own bed rather than a hotel room. The 5-foot-10 guard, who has been nicknamed "Energizer Bunny" by Rockets' telecaster Bill Worrell, owns a home in the L.A. area and lives there during the off-season.

Brooks was beginning to feel like his old self in Seattle, though the vicious bug had left him weak. He dressed out, but didn't play. Now, he's hoping to make his return from a three-game hiatus tomorrow against Minnesota.

"I'm ready. What'd Rudy say?" an anxious Brooks said after going through his first light practice in a week.

The Rockets need the Energizer Bunny back in the lineup. Houston is 12–0 this season and 31–3 over two years when Brooks plays the entire fourth quarter. There were a couple of second-quarter unravelings at Phoenix and Seattle, and Brooks is a stabilizer who generally won't allow his team to go into the doldrums for sustained stretches.

One of the best things the Rockets ever did was steal Brooks from Minnesota for a second-round draft choice. He is such an attribute to the organization, both on the court and off.

He's not big. He's not particularly fast. But he has a heart as big as Texas and truly appreciates that he is living a dream by playing in the NBA.

If kids are indeed going to look up to pro athletes as role models, I can only hope my 8-year-old son will try to emulate the basic qualities of a Scott Brooks. This is a warm, caring person off the court and a fierce competitor who gets everything out of his ability while in the workplace.

Brooks has told me he developed his work ethic and humanistic values from his mother, who raised a large family in California by herself.

She truly did a great job with young Scott. He's a winner through and through, a classic overachiever who some day will make a great coach at the college or professional level.

But let me quickly descend from my Scott Brooks soapbox and get back to the issue at hand.

The Rockets have arrived in frigid Minneapolis with a healthy, complete cast of players. Maybe Brooks will be able to help this team ring out the old year in style.

December 30

Tomjanovich decided to hold Brooks out until the club gets home. There's a four-day break between games, and Brooks will be able to get in a couple of hard scrimmages before taking his place in the rotation.

As it turned out, Houston didn't need the little guy tonight against the Timberwolves.

Olajuwon, Thorpe and Bullard were masterful as Houston closed out the road trip 2–2 with a 110–104 victory. Hakeem had 34 points, Thorpe was rock-solid in the trenches with 20 points and 17 rebounds, and Bullard came off the bench to hit 5 of 6 shots.

Happy New Year. Despite a shaky week, Houston, 24–4, has come to the end of the '93 portion of the schedule with more wins than any team in the league. Even more impressively, 17 of its 28 games have been on the road. After Jan. 15, the club will be able to settle in for a long winter's home stretch. Thus, getting all these road games out of the way early could be the difference in the race for the No. 1 playoff seed in the West.

"This was a big victory for us," Tomjanovich said. "I was really worried coming in at the end of a long road trip, but we finished it off."

Any New Year's resolutions for the coach?

"Lose weight, not games," Tomjanovich quipped.

It was a night to hold the cheeseburgers and order something special from Olajuwon, Thorpe and Bullard.

CHAPTER THREE

The Struggle: January–March

January 1, 1994

Of all the NBA rules, the one I like best is this: Practice is prohibited on New Year's Day.

A couple of years ago, before Tomjanovich took over, the Rockets weren't aware of this golden rule and practiced on New Year's. They promptly got socked with a $10,000 fine. And then they went out and got beat the next night, proving that practice doesn't make perfect.

Since the team isn't practicing today, I get to be a couch potato from the Cotton Bowl to the Orange Bowl. But somewhere between Lou Holtz and Charlie Ward, my mind wanders to a conversation I had last week in Seattle with Ray Melchiorre, the Rockets' trainer.

Melchiorre is the only man on the Rockets' bench who has been part of a world championship team. He was the Celtics' trainer when Boston won titles in 1981, 1984 and 1986.

I asked Melchiorre if there were similarities between this Rockets' team and those Boston title teams that Melchiorre came to know and love.

"I really think there are," Melchoirre said. "The thing I'm noticing this year is a more businesslike approach in practice. That's the way those Boston teams were.

"The players seem very respectful of each other. They don't only listen when a coach makes a point. They also pay attention if a teammate has something to interject. That's what I mean by being businesslike."

The Celtics of the '80s were built around a superstar named Larry Bird. This Rockets' team is built around a superstar named Olajuwon.

"We certainly have the great main man, as the Celtics did with Bird," Melchiorre said. "The supporting people all have done a good job in their roles, which was the case in Boston, too. In both cases, you're talking about very cohesive teams."

As a new calender year begins, I can only wonder if those similarities will hold up through winter and spring.

January 4

Here we are in January and Les Alexander still hasn't come up with a general manager replacement for Patterson. This is what you call a cruise control front office.

Leiweke has been spearheading the delicate search, saying he wanted someone who could be compatible both with Tomjanovich and Alexander. Leiweke tried to recruit former NBA standpoint Len Elmore, who has a law degree and a highly successful sports-agent business. Elmore, while flattered, turned the Rockets down because of the commitment to his business.

Various other people have been lobbying for the basketball operations position, but nothing has really been hot.

Until tonight.

Jerry Reynolds, the interim Sacramento general manager, showed up at The Summit and was seen in the Board Room after the Rockets' victory over Portland. A couple of weeks ago, Kings owner Jim Thomas had announced the team would be searching for a new GM.

Reynolds would stay on in Sacramento until a replacement was named.

Hmmmm. Could it be the Rockets finally had their man?

Reynolds didn't win many games in Sacramento, but many league observers felt he was a knowledgeable, hard-working personnel man who had simply been the victim of former owner Gregg Luckenbill's ineptitude.

If the Rockets are about to hire Reynolds, the timing is certainly right. The trading deadline is Feb. 24. All teams need a general manager in place during that time, in case there are opportunities to improve the club.

I'm told Reynolds was invited to Houston by Alexander. The two are supposed to have a meeting in the morning. Stay tuned.

January 5

How bad are the Dallas Mavericks? So bad that the loudest ovation from the sparse Reunion Arena crowd is reserved for front-row spectator Emmitt Smith of the Cowboys.

Smith came to tonight's game, ostensibly to see Maxwell, an old Florida buddy.

Maxwell went 0 for 8 from the floor. Since he couldn't score a basket for the Dallas running back, he gave Smith a Rockets' jersey at the end of Houston's 114–102 victory.

Rockets' people are starting to get a bit concerned about Maxwell's shooting slump. Since his memorable buzzer-beater at San Antonio a couple of weeks ago, Maxwell has seen his field-goal percentage slip from .438 to .390. He can't get the proper lift for his jump shot because of tendinitis in both knees.

"When I jump, it feels like somebody is hitting me in the knees with a hammer," Maxwell said. "I've been stinking it up, but as long as the team is winning, I'm happy."

January 6

At the Dallas airport this morning, I asked Rudy his opinion of Reynolds and whether he thought Reynolds would fit well in the Rockets' basketball structure. Tomjanovich indicated he felt Reynolds would be a good candidate for the key operations position.

I was told later in the day that the meeting between Les Alexander and Reynolds went well. Reynolds headed back to California, and I was able to reach him by telephone.

"I'll admit I was in Houston," said Reynolds, who is known for having a keen sense of humor. "I'll go anywhere to see a good basketball game, even if it's halfway across the country."

Although Reynolds couldn't say anything specific, I could tell the idea of joining a 26–4 team greatly intrigued him.

The 30-game juncture for Houston was an anniversary of sorts. Last year at the 30-game mark, Houston hit rock bottom at 14–16. The club had lost seven in a row. What a difference a calendar year makes.

A year ago at this time, Maxwell was questioning the team's toughness, Tomjanovich was turning down his car radio to avoid hearing the negative comments, and club management was wondering which would come first, a Rockets' victory or Valentine's Day.

"To look at where we are this year after 30 games and where we were last year after 30 games . . . it's unbelievable," Brooks said. "You're talking about basically the same players now as then. But we showed character and jelled into a true team."

Since the 30-game mark last year, Houston's cumulative regular-season record is 67–15.

"I knew that, deep down, we had pride and potential," Maxwell reflected. "But we had to make a new commitment to defense. Once we began accepting the fact that defense wins games, we became a hard ballclub for teams to deal with."

January 7

Ring, ring.

I was still on my first cup of coffee this morning when the office called to inform me Vernon is in the hospital. He had complained of an irregular heartbeat last night, and his wife drove him to Methodist Hospital. There, he was diagnosed as having cardiac arrhythmia and put on medication.

Anytime there's a heart-related problem in basketball these days, everybody has a tendency to think about the recent deaths of Hank Gathers and Reggie Lewis. But sometimes, fibrillation episodes occur—for no apparent reason—and there are no further problems after the heart converts to its normal rhythm.

Olajuwon missed six games in 1991 after suffering an atrial fibrillation episode. He has had no heart problems since.

The Rockets are going to take every precaution with Maxwell, who said he was feeling much better late in the day.

There will be no attempt to put him on the basketball court again until he feels completely comfortable doing so. In the meantime, Elie will move into the starting lineup, with Cassell rejoining the rotation as a backup guard.

When it comes to matters of the heart, you take no chances. The hope is that Maxwell's fibrillation problem will be minor, as Olajuwon's was in '91.

In the meantime, the Rockets must press on without their emotional leader, who just might be the No. 2 player on this team in terms of value.

January 8

So far, so good without Maxwell.

The Rockets received 19 points from Elie and 16 from Cassell in a 100–93 victory over Philadelphia at The Summit. That's what you call picking up the slack at the big-guard spot.

Meanwhile, there was more encouraging news on the Maxwell situation.

Dr. Walter Lowe, one of the club's physicians, was at the game tonight and said Maxwell had been released from the hospital. Lowe said Maxwell was doing fine and scheduled for a stress test. If the test goes well, the doctors will clear Maxwell to rejoin the team for at least a portion of the upcoming road trip.

I'm wondering about Vernon's mental outlook when he does get back.

Even for a guy as tough as Maxwell, an atrial fibrillation episode has to be a scary situation. Taking a stress test under the watchful eye of some of the finest doctors in the world is one thing. But will there be a mental barrier when it comes time to sprint down a basketball floor for the first time since the incident?

This upcoming trip to Orlando, Boston, Washington and Chicago will be challenging. If Maxwell isn't ready, either physically or mentally, the Rockets may be served a huge dose of humility.

January 10

Two national television appearances, two blowout losses.

The casual airchair fans across the country must be wondering if the Rockets are a camera-shy aggregation. Remember how Houston embarrassed itself on NBC back on Christmas Day? Well, tonight the Rockets blew up on TNT.

The Rockets might have anticipated that O'Neal and Hardaway would have big outings for Orlando. But who would have imagined that old buddy Tree Rollins would bite the hand which once fed him?

Rollins apparently had finished his playing career with the Rockets last year. Tomjanovich wanted him to join the Houston coaching staff, but the protracted sale of the club resulted in Rollins taking a coaching job with Orlando.

But tonight, with the Magic desperate for backup center help, the 38-year-old Rollins was activated. He held his own in the trenches for eight minutes and provided an inspirational lift that helped the Magic beat Houston by 15 points.

"There were no butterflies," Rollins deadpanned. "At my age, all the butterflies are dead."

January 11

After last night's game at Orlando Arena, I approached Hakeem as he was putting on his street clothes.

"There's only one arena in this league where you've never won," I said.

"Where's that?"

"Boston."

"Really?"

Just a little food for thought.

I don't figure Hakeem is going 0-for-a-career in the fabled Garden, the leprechauns notwithstanding. Logic dictates that this should be the year for Olajuwon to break through. The Celtics stink, and the Rockets will be hankering to atone for the Orlando loss.

Houston's last regular-season win in Boston Garden came early in the 1981–82 season when a young center named Moses Malone scored 37 points in a 106–104 Rockets victory. Since then, the Rockets have been New England's whipping boys.

When Olajuwon made his first trip to Boston Garden in 1984, he was given a tour of the historic building by Rockets' officials. At the end of the tour, Olajuwon gave his guides a good laugh.

"This place," Olajuwon concluded, "is a dump."

Yeah, and the Rockets have been pure garbage while playing in that dump.

Tomorrow, the parquet jinx should end. Finally.

January 12

Vernon's back.

He flew to Boston late last night and media members were flocking toward him as he laced up his sneakers 90 minutes before tip-off.

"Let me work out first," Maxwell said, "then I'll talk to everybody."

Maxwell shot and ran for short intervals. Between sessions, strength coach Robert Barr would check Maxwell's pulse. After the 15-minute workout, Maxwell came back into the locker room with a shaken look on his face. Clearly, he was not psychologically ready to play. And when Boston media members kept reminding Maxwell he had been on the court where Lewis collapsed, it didn't make the situation any lighter.

Maxwell said he felt uncomfortable as he was finishing the workout, complaining of a lightheaded feeling.

"I only have one life," Maxwell said. "There's no second chance once you're gone. All the doctors have said my heart is fine, and they've cleared me. But I'm going to take it slow."

With Maxwell sitting, the Rockets won anyway to break the 11-game regular-season losing streak at Boston Garden. Boston had plenty of heroes in the stands . . . legends like Auerbach and John Havlicek. But alas, there were no Boston heroes on the court.

Olajuwon outscored Robert Parish 37–0, and the Rockets could finally smile into the Garden rafters, where the Celtics' leprechaun supposedly resides.

"The leprechaun took the year off," Celtics forward Xavier McDaniel said glumly. "I guess he's on vacation."

January 13

Here we go again with CharterGate.

The players have expressed an undercurrent of frustration all season long because they believe other teams have a travel advantage with either exclusive charter travel or charters on all back-to-back trips.

Tonight, all the venom became public after Houston was walloped 120–102 by the lowly Washington Bullets.

Everybody was ticked off because Houston didn't charter out immediately after the Boston game. With that travel itinerary, the Rockets could have slept in at their Maryland hotel and had a midday preparation meeting to dissect the Bullets' strengths and weaknesses.

Instead, Houston had to rise early, take a commercial flight to Baltimore and a bus to its Maryland hotel. Arriving around 1 p.m., there was time only for a quick nap before the trip to the game.

"We should have been here," said co-captain Olajuwon, speaking on behalf of the team. "We should have been able to sleep in and watch film. They say every back-to-back is a charter. I don't know why this trip wasn't a charter. That's not an excuse for losing the game, but it's a big factor."

Olajuwon said if the Alexander regime truly believes the Rockets can go all the way, it should provide the club with every opportunity to go into a game physically and mentally prepared.

"If you cut corners, you pay the price," Olajuwon said. "Was the reason we didn't charter to save money? I don't know."

With all the travel furor, Maxwell's return became a footnote. He played 20 minutes and scored 10 points. Good to see him break that psychological barrier. Max should be OK from now on.

January 14

Les Alexander must have been reading the papers this morning because damage control is under way.

En route to Chicago, the players were informed that club management has decreed that all back-to-back games the remainder of the season will involve charter trips.

Ta-da. Do a little arm-twisting and ye shall receive.

January 15

The Good Ship Rockets has hit some choppy waters.

Tonight's 82–76 loss to Chicago was an ugly offensive struggle and left several players in a foul mood. There's nothing like a 1–3 road trip to stir the second-guessers. Thorpe didn't quite understand why Herrera finished at power forward, and starters Horry and Smith weren't doing handsprings over their 16- and 23-minute stints, respectively.

The thing is, Houston is still in great shape with a 28–7 record, considering that 22 of the 35 games have been played on the road. Basically, I just think the Rockets have finally been worn down by the relentless road schedule.

Tomjanovich had the same thought.

"I don't like losing this game, but I'm happy as hell with where we are after 35 games, especially considering our schedule," Tomjanovich said. "This league is too good to just roll right through it. Every good team is going to have to weather two or three storms."

But a storm naturally breeds frustration among the troops, and Rudy will have to deal with some of that.

This is why the NBA is a fascinating enterprise. A team can be flying high one week and down in the doldrums the next.

Even Pat Riley recently said the league is good enough to bring even the best team to its knees three or four times a year.

I'm eager to see how the Rockets react now that they're finally having a little adversity.

January 16

After a week on the road, most of the Rockets' players, coaches and support staff members couldn't wait to get home. They arose early in Chicago, braved the minus 7 degrees temperature and made it to O'Hare Airport for the morning's first non-stop flight to Houston.

The second wave showed up at the airport a few hours later. Rudy, Smith and Horry were there, and I managed to sneak up to the small first-class cabin with that trio. As the plane takes off, I'm beginning to feel some bad vibrations. Horry has a forlorn look before grabbing a pillow and falling asleep. Smith is quiet throughout the trip.

I know these guys aren't happy about their recent playing time, and I'm wondering if this is going to become a serious issue should the team continue to struggle. After a 22–1 start, Houston has gone a mediocre 6–6 since Dec. 23.

Anyway, I can't wait for this plane to land so I can hurry home and watch the Oilers-Kansas City playoff game. Nearly everybody in Houston has Super Bowl Fever. After a 1–4 start, the Oilers are riding into the playoffs with an 11-game winning streak.

If the Oilers win today, few people are going to care about the Rockets—at least for another week. Houstonians crave a first major sports championship, and it looks like the Oilers are primed to give it to them.

January 17

Well, so much for that crazy notion that Houston might soon become a city of champions.

The Oilers fell under Joe Montana's magic spell yesterday and now everybody's into the familiar lament: Same old Houston. Can't win the big one. Can't break that championship jinx.

It would be nice if all those deflated fans would hop on the Rockets' bandwagon, but I'm not sure they can open their hearts to any sports franchise right now. This Oilers thing hurt too much.

Besides, the Rockets haven't done anything lately to win the fans' trust. With the Spurs having won six in a row to move with 3 games of first place in the Midwest Division, Houston needs to get well tomorrow night at home against Boston.

Tough times for football and basketball. How many more days until the Astros begin spring training?

January 18

The Rockets' woes continued tonight during a 95–83 loss to the sad-sack Celtics at The Summit. You know things are going poorly when 40-year-old Robert Parish can act like Ponce de Leon at the Fountain of Youth.

Parish—who had been shut out by the Rockets just a week earlier—exploded for 19 points and 17 rebounds. Other than Olajuwon and Thorpe, Houston's offense has hit the skids. Maxwell continues to be in a horrid shooting slump, and Smith and Horry are nowhere. Smith played 22 minutes tonight and hit 2 of 7 shots. Horry played 19 minutes and was 1 of 5.

When three starters are spinning their wheels—for whatever reasons—it doesn't take a Hoopology major to recognize there's going to be a lack of overall production.

With the tension continuing to build, I figured it was time to talk to a frustrated Smith about what was going on.

All the other players had left the locker room when Smith began to discuss his situation. The conversation was intended for background only, not for publication. Smith felt Rudy had been giving him too quick of a hook, which was, in turn, affecting his performance. But the point guard wasn't ready to say anthing in print which might be perceived as rocking the boat. This was, after all, just a minor team slump and maybe the situation would quickly rectify itself.

These matters are always delicate. It's like the chicken-and-egg subject. The player says he needs minutes to perform well. The coach says the minutes will come if the performance is satisfactory.

I simply filed the information in my memory bank and headed for the parking garage.

January 19

Saddled with their first three-game losing streak in more than a year, the Rockets went behind closed doors for a team meeting today. Tomjanovich offered candid analysis of problem areas and players were encouraged to offer opinions about why the Rockets are 6–7 over the last 13 games.

"We have some unhappy guys because we've lost three games in a row," Brooks said. "To me, that's a healthy sign. It shows that guys care. I've been on a Minnesota team that lost 15 in a row before anybody decided to call a meeting."

Nobody was talking about the specifics of the meeting. But I have to believe the Smith/Horry issues were addressed. In the past three games, Horry has played 13, 16 and 19 minutes, scoring zero, five and four points. Smith has played 23, 23 and 22 minutes, scoring six, five and five points.

Maxwell's jumper is on vacation, and Elie can't shoot the ball well because of that chipped bone in his right hand. I reiterate: If Smith, Horry and Maxwell aren't contributing to this offense, there *is* no offense.

I was typing a story on the team meeting when Les Alexander walked into the press room and invited the *Houston Chronicle*'s Eddie Sefko and me to lunch. We went to Carrabba's on Kirby, thinking that maybe Alexander had something important to tell us.

He didn't.

We asked how life as an NBA owner was treating him.

"Lots of bills," lamented Les. "It seems like all I do is open bills."

He admitted he had made a mistake hiring a controller shortly after taking over the club. He said the person had been promptly dismissed because the job had proven overwhelming and that a search was ongoing for a new controller.

That was about it.

When we got back to The Summit, Sefko and I looked at each other with quizzical expressions and simultaneously asked the same question:

"What was that all about?"

January 20

I think I've got a much better idea now why Les Alexander invited the beat writers for that public relations lunch yesterday. He must have been softening us up for the bombshell he would knew would be hitting the news today.

Jay Goldberg, the Rockets' media information director, called me at the Denver City Center Marriott this morning.

"Leiweke is in Denver," Goldberg said. "He's staying at the Westin and needs to talk to you. You're not going to believe this. It's going to floor you."

As soon as I hung up with Goldberg, I called Leiweke.

"I'm leaving the Rockets," Leiweke said. "I'm going back to work for the Warriors. I'll be spearheading the project to get the Warriors a new arena."

Goldberg had been right. The news floored me.

"We'd better talk about this face-to-face," I suggested to Leiweke, who invited me right over.

I walked the three city blocks to the Westin and wound up spending an hour in Leiweke's room.

Although I pressed hard for Leiweke to reveal the *real* reason why he would leave a prestigious job as club president of an NBA team, he initially stuck pretty much to the party line.

"I left my heart in San Francisco," Leiweke insisted.

The downcast expression on his face suggested otherwise, and it soon became apparent that philosophical differences had cropped up between Leiweke and Alexander. A guy doesn't give up an executive job with the PGA Tour in Florida, pop into Houston for four months and then promptly call the moving vans unless there have been some problems at the office.

For Tomjanovich and the basketball staff, this would be represent another serious blow to the organization's overall stability. First Patterson, now Leiweke.

In his short tenure, Leiweke had fought for the basketball people on various matters. He had become extremely fond of Tomjanovich and vice versa.

The Rockets' front office was already in turmoil, with many employees from the old Patterson regime either being fired or resigning to take a job with Patterson's new sports venture. Steve had become involved in bringing an International Hockey League franchise to Houston.

The joke is that you need a scorecard to tell who works in the Rockets' front office from week to week. And the irony is that Leiweke has come to empathize with Patterson—the man he had replaced in September.

"I met Steve at a party one night, and I think he felt like punching me in the face," Leiweke said. "You know what? If I had been him, I would have punched me in the face, too."

John Thomas, who had just joined the Rockets as a Leiweke hire, would be stepping up to inherit Leiweke's job as head of business operations.

Back on the court, things were no less tumultuous.

In the Mile High altitude, the Rockets reached the low point of their season. They blew a seemingly safe seven-point lead with 1:52 left in the first overtime and wound up losing 111–106 in double overtime. It was Houston's fourth defeat in a row.

What a day. You would have sworn the whole organization was going up in smoke.

January 21

I was in the sleepy-head, second wave of travelers again. After the Denver-to-Houston flight landed at Intercontinental Airport, I happened to run into Smith and his father in the Terminal C concourse.

I don't think Kenny was seeking me out. But after a few seconds of small talk, he said it was time to go on the record regarding his lack of playing time. Last night against Denver, he had played only 23 of a possible 58 minutes. With the Rockets' guards playing on wobbly legs in the second overtime, Houston had managed only three points in the five-minute session.

And still, Smith sat. Apparently, that galling loss convinced him it was time to make his frustrations known to the public.

I pulled out my pen and pad and the basic points Smith had made earlier in the week after the Boston game were reinforced—this time on the record.

"I don't think my abilities are being respected," Smith said. "I've made big shots in this league . . . in big games. I don't think anybody could play well under these circumstances. We're almost halfway through the season now, and the issue has to be addressed.

"For me to play better, I have to have the opportunity. Right now, I'm sort of in-between. It's important for me to get a rhythm and be in the flow of the game. I'm the kind of guy—if I'm 2 for 7—I can hit my next three shots and be 5 for 10.

"It's a little tough for me right now. . . . For this team to reach its full potential, I have to do some things to give us better offensive balance. You have to have the perimeter threats out there."

Rudy had taken the early flight on an off-day. When I got home, I called to let him know Smith had broached the subject of playing time.

The coach knew this wasn't a case of a reporter coercing a player into making controversial remarks. Rudy didn't want to get into a public rebuttal with Smith through the media, but it was my job to make that response opportunity available.

"I just didn't want you to pick up the paper and read it without knowing what was going on," I said.

"I understand," Tomjanovich replied. "Thanks."

January 22

Finally, some positive news.

After Smith talked the talk, he walked the walk. One day after his plea for more playing time, Smith got a 36-minute green light from Tomjanovich as the Rockets came off Skid Row with a 106–101 victory over Utah.

Olajuwon was dominant with a 40-point night, but Mr. Inside needed some help from Mr. Outside. After five consecutive single-digit scoring games, Smith came through with 19 points, including 15 in the second half.

"I'm happy as hell for him," Tomjanovich said. "Kenny made the statements and put pressure on himself. He was playing well . . .

pumped up. I gave the guy a chance to prove himself down the stretch, and he came through."

Smith didn't mind putting pressure on himself because the alternative wasn't working. He felt he had nothing to lose.

"Getting into the flow of the game is very important to me, and I did that tonight," Smith said. "I got the opportunity. All I wanted to do was bring my situation to light without disrupting the chemistry of the team."

But just as one hole was temporarily plugged, the Rockets sprang a leak somewhere else.

Horry played only 18 minutes, continuing his trend as a starter who plays less time than his backup. He contributed only two points and had no rebounds.

A sullen Horry left the Rockets' locker room in a huff when asked what was wrong with his game.

"I haven't been out there that much," he shot back while ambling down the hallway. "Maybe there's a trade fixing to come down. I don't care. Business is business."

January 23

Les Alexander has turned his attention from Jerry Reynolds to Portland personnel man Brad Greenberg in the never-ending search for a vice president of basketball operations.

Don't ask me why.

I checked with a Blazers' insider who told me the Portland coaches were keeping their fingers crossed that Greenberg would go to Houston. The Portland coaches believe Greenberg is an enemy to them, not a friend. The word is, Head Coach Rick Adelman would consider it a tremendous bonus if he could get Greenberg out of his hair.

It's roughly a month before the trading deadline, and the Rockets have nobody in place to talk with other clubs about deals or explain the ramifications of the salary cap. And with Leiweke gone, there's nobody to serve as a buffer between Rudy and Les.

If I could take a crash course in Salary Cap 101, I might apply for the six-figure opening.

After today's practice, all the pent-up frustration that Horry has felt over the past few weeks poured out of him like water going over Niagara Falls. KTRH radio's Rich Lord was there, and the writers gathered around as the usually soft-spoken Horry let it all go.

Horry said he felt like a "backup starter" who was being teased by Tomjanovich.

"I need the minutes to get involved in the game," Horry said. "Without the minutes, there's no Robert Horry. Right now, I feel I have no role. I feel lost."

Over the last six games, Horry has averaged just 3.0 points in 20.6 minutes.

"It doesn't make any sense," Horry said. "I wouldn't tease a guy like that. Either you're going to play him or you're not going to play him. Don't even start a guy if you're going to tease him."

Horry suggested that if the minutes distribution didn't change, perhaps Tomjanovich should start Elie at small forward.

"If you're going to play me 18 minutes—and the guy backing me up is playing more minutes—bump that," Horry said. "The guy getting the most minutes should be the starter. I figure he should start Mario and let me give Mario a rest. Then I'll go out there and give you 18 minutes of hard work."

Horry had a premonition the Rockets would try to move him before the trading deadline.

"I love my teammates, the coaching staff . . . everything is cool," Horry said. "But when game time comes, I feel like my minutes are vanishing, depleted. Pretty soon, I see myself either out of here or the 12th man."

Horry's lack of playing time had been a result of his failure to take an aggressive offensive approach. The coaching staff had been talking with Horry about that sore subject, encouraging him to take the spot-up shot when his man sags off on Olajuwon.

"For me, I can't really take that shot," Horry said. "You have no rhythm to get it off. It's like eating steak with plastic on your tongue. If you want me to get my shots, I have to come off some picks and get a little rhythm."

The media then went traipsing down the hall to knock on Tomjanovich's office door and explain that a second player in four days had publicly questioned the dispersal of playing time.

"The only way you can get out of a situation is to work hard, bust your butt and good things will happen," Tomjanovich said. "I want my guys to be happy, but my job is to win ballgames. I don't expect people to always be happy with playing time. If anybody thinks these things are personal . . . I'm not like that."

Last month, I thought coaching the Rockets was an ideal job. Today, I'm beginning to think it's an impossible job.

January 25

Maxwell is the Rockets' version of Harry Houdini. Max mesmerized his Summit audience with another great escape tonight.

Houston trailed Cleveland 93–91 when Maxwell reared up for a three-pointer at the 29-second mark that proved to be the definitive shot of the game.

"I was either going to be a hero or a zero," Maxwell said.

Big, big win. Considering all the flap about playing time recently, the locker room could have been a haven for the amateur shrinks if the Rockets had lost.

The Rockets are 30–9, a half-game behind Seattle for best record in the West. Their leader doesn't want to hear any more chatter about playing time.

"We are in a unique position," Olajuwon said. "If people are going to complain, we may as well get ready for the summer. A win like this can help bring us together. But the key is to stay together, because we are going to be tested in so many areas as this season goes along."

If the Rockets can win their next two games, there's a good chance Tomjanovich and his staff will be coaching the Western Conference All-Star team.

Great. Then he'll have a whole batch of blue-chippers clamoring for playing time.

Horry may be in line for the Jeanne Dixon crystal ball award.

He had predicted last week the Rockets were going to trade him and today a rumor has surfaced about an Horry-for-Sean Elliott deal with the Pistons. Immediately, I had a flashback to that Monday diatribe by Horry and the subsequent march to Tomjanovich's office. Just as Tomjanovich answered the knock on his door, the coach was informed he had a call from Detroit personnel director Billy McKinney.

"Billy, I've got the press in my office," Tomjanovich had said. "I'll get right back with you."

I didn't think anything about it at the time.

But after hearing this rumor, I'm now putting 2-and-2 together in my mind. Did that Tomjanovich-McKinney conversation five days ago start the ball rolling for a changing of the small forwards?

When told about the circulating rumor, Tomjanovich reiterated his policy never to discuss trade speculation.

The Rockets needed a victory over Indiana coupled with a Seattle home-court loss to New York to make Tomjanovich the coach of the Western Conference All-Stars. But the resurgent Indiana Pacers made sure Tomjanovich would be in the stands rather than on the court during All-Star Weekend in Minneapolis.

The Pacers shot a sizzling .608 from the floor as Houston's defense turned soft as a marshmallow.

"This was a great example of coming out half-stepping and getting kicked square in the butt," Tomjanovich said.

Horry played 35 minutes. Wonder if the Rockets were showcasing him?

The Brad Greenberg scare is over.

Tonight in Portland, Greenberg told the Blazers' media he has withdrawn his name from consideration for the Rockets' vice president of basketball operations job. Greenberg cited "philosophical differences" with Alexander.

The real story, I'm told, is that Greenberg wanted total control over basketball operations, including the power to hire and fire coaches. There's no way Rudy was going to stand for that kind of arrangement.

I have to believe Rudy put his foot down with Les after checking out Greenberg through league sources.

The Rockets are now back at Square One in their search for a vice president of basketball operations. First of all, they need to write down the job description so there is no confusion. Everybody knows Rudy is going to have the final word on all personnel decisions.

So, this job isn't going to be a traditional general manager's job.

The job is for someone who can cultivate league sources, deal with agents, analyze the salary cap and generally provide Tomjanovich with the research to make the best possible personnel decisions.

Alexander can forget about getting somebody in place before the trading deadline.

If the Rockets are going to make any deals before Feb. 24, Rudy will have to do all the research on his own.

January 31

Before flying to Salt Lake City this afternoon, I decided to check a little deeper into this Horry/Elliott trade rumor. If the Rockets weren't going to say anything, maybe somebody on the Pistons' end would.

John Harris, the Pistons' writer for Booth Newspapers, is on my notes network conference call each week and the network people always trade information. I called John and asked him if he could probe the Detroit people on this topic after tonight's Pistons-Cleveland game.

After arriving in Salt Lake, former Rockets coach Tom Nissalke invited a group of media types—myself, Peterson, director of communications Jim Foley and Channel 20 producer Paul Byckowski—to his restaurant, Greenstreet. When I got back to the hotel, my red message light was blinking.

The message was from Harris. He said a high-ranking Pistons' official had confirmed the Horry/Elliott trade was definitely brewing. I immediately called Harris at The Palace, and he gave me his source's quote.

"Right now, it's close," the source said. "It's a perfect match in terms of the salary cap and what each team needs. We would have to take two players from Houston and give up one."

Harris said the Pistons' official was extremely excited about the possible acquisition of Horry. Recently retired center Bill Laimbeer had walked up during the conversation, and the official seemed to want Laimbeer to leave so the trade topic could be further explored with Harris.

With only 15 minutes until deadline, I wrote a quick story for *The Houston Post* that said a 2-for-1 deal was in the works.

Looks like the Rockets are going to roll the dice and dramatically alter the chemistry of a 31–10 team.

February 1

I ran into Rockets telecaster Bill Worrell in the lobby of the Salt Lake Marriott this morning and asked him what he thought about a possible Horry for Elliott deal.

Worrell grimaced. He wasn't keen on the idea of giving up Horry, a second-year player with a world of athletic ability. Bill talked about the defensive implications of an Horry departure. This was a Rockets team that had become a winner because of its defensive personality. Horry had been in a malaise, granted. But when the Rockets are rolling defensively, Horry always seems to be a big part of the equation. He can defend both the big and small forwards. He can steal the ball, block shots and rebound better than Elliott.

I agreed with Worrell that Houston couldn't possibly be as good defensively if the trade goes through. The flip side of the issue, of course, is that maybe the Rockets wouldn't have to be such defensive terrors if Elliott could provide Houston with a second major offensive weapon behind Olajuwon.

Before tonight's Rockets-Jazz game, I called Patterson to ask about the salary-cap ramifications of this trade. Turns out, I hadn't been the only one seeking salary-cap advice.

With nobody in the Rockets' front office to provide salary-cap expertise, the Rockets' coaches had called Patterson the previous week to determine how a deal could be put together.

Elliott is approximately a $1.8 million player for cap purposes and Horry is about $1.2 million. Thus, the second Rockets player in the deal must have a salary in the $600,000 range. There are only two possibilities: Brooks and Bullard. Houston wouldn't give up Brooks at this juncture, so Bullard has to be the second player in the deal by process of elimination.

As the Rockets are being pummeled 104–88 by the Jazz, I'm thinking about the incredible loyalty and character of Steve Patterson.

For him to still offer his salary-cap counseling to the coaches after being fired by Alexander last August is a noble thing, indeed.

I'm also thinking about Patterson's assertion that the trade didn't add up. Patterson smelled a rat, saying he would be concerned about taking a player like Elliott, who was being shopped for the second time in a four-month span.

Bottom line, the Rockets could be vulnerable to making a bad trade right now because they don't have a general manager like Patterson to give the coaching staff a detached, unemotional perspective.

It's the old deal about being so close to the forest, you can't see the trees.

The solution isn't necessarily bringing in a big-name scorer at the expense of your best young asset. A less-risky solution would be getting Smith untracked and getting Maxwell out of his shooting slump. When the guards come back and reach their scoring potential, the team won't have to worry that much about instant offense at small forward.

Then you can preserve Horry's all-round game and vast potential for improvement.

This proposed Elliott trade will be popular on the call-in radio shows, but I'm not convinced at this point it will make Houston a better ballclub.

February 2

At baggage claim back in Houston, Tomjanovich looked weary as he waited for his luggage.

"A little R & R today?" I asked.

"We'll see," Tomjanovich said with a sigh.

My suspicion was that there would be no rest and recuperation for the man who was having to not only coach the team, but do all the exhausting legwork on the rumored blockbuster trade.

One thing is certain: If Rudy is going to make this deal, you can bet he will check out every aspect of Elliott's game and know everything there is to know about Elliott's character. Nobody works harder than Tomjanovich and his staff.

There are also financial implications here that Les Alexander will have to handle. Elliott's total compensation is about $2.8 million, and he'll be a restricted free agent at the end of the year. It's only common sense that Houston would have to lock in Elliott long-term before it could sign off on a trade.

Elliott would likely be looking for around $3 million annually.

I'm wondering if Alexander is willing to shell out that kind of money.

February 3

A deal is imminent.

Berk Kinerk, the agent for Elliott, confirmed before tonight's Rockets-Lakers game that Elliott is on the verge of becoming a Rocket, pending final contract extension negotiations with Alexander.

"Basically, the Rockets expressed they want to make the deal," Kinerk said. "The personnel has been defined. Both sides want to do this, but there are some loose financial ends to be tied down."

Horry played 20 minutes in what may have been his last Houston game. The Rockets were sloppy but won 99–88.

"Nobody has said anything to me about it (a trade), so I'm not going to worry about it," Horry said. "But if it happens, I told you so."

February 4

The trade was announced at midmorning. Horry and Bullard were ushered into meetings with Tomjanovich as soon as they arrived at The Summit.

"This is the hardest thing I've had to do since becoming the head coach of this team," Tomjanovich said. "I have strong, strong feelings for both Robert and Matt. But it's my evaluation that we're adding a quality player and a quality person. It's not what Robert and Matt didn't do, it's what Sean Elliott *can* do."

The remaining Rockets didn't take it well at all. Players were not happy that their "family" had been broken up. But keep in mind the Rockets haven't been acting like much of a family. They're 10–10 over the last 20 games, and there has been some finger pointing and cop-out excuses.

After getting the news from Tomjanovich, Horry and Bullard met for a final time with the Houston media.

"I think they got some pressure from up above," Horry said. "It has been a messed-up situation since we got new ownership. As soon as an All-Star like Sean Elliott becomes available—boom—forget the young person who can grow and make the team better down the line."

Added Bullard: "It's strange that a team could go 22–1 and get to the point where it's at now—where people are starting to panic a little bit. But that's just the way the league is. It's a tough league, and it's hard to maintain intensity for 82 games. I guess this was just something the Rockets felt they needed to do."

Horry and Bullard gathered their belongings and headed for the elevator.

It was as though a pall had been cast over The Summit. Breaking up is hard to do.

February 5

The plan was for Elliott to take his Rockets physical this morning, have a news conference and join the team for a 5 p.m. workout. I was taking the day off, but happened to flip on KTRH radio and hear the perplexing news that Elliott had been told to wait indefinitely at Stouffer's Presidente Hotel while doctors were evaluating his exam.

The process stretched on and on . . . into the evening hours. The Rockets weren't shedding any light on the subject, but KTRH reported the medical investigation dealt with an Elliott kidney problem.

Meanwhile, in Auburn Hill, Mich., Horry and Bullard were being told by the Pistons they couldn't suit up for the Detroit-New Jersey game because Elliott had not yet passed his physical.

The Rockets finally said the fact-finding mission would be continued tomorrow.

Crazy stuff.

I'm glad I wasn't on duty today.

February 6

I got a call at home around 1 p.m. The deal was off, and the Rockets had scheduled a 3 p.m. news conference to explain why.

Initially, there wasn't a lot of explaining. The Rockets simply said Elliott had flunked his physical. Horry and Bullard would be rejoining the Rockets, and Elliott would go back to Detroit.

The Trade That Wasn't.

"It's an unfortunate situation," Tomjanovich said. "I feel for all the parties involved."

It took awhile to piece together what really happened. But basically, the Rockets' physicians had a different interpretation of Elliott's kidney problem than the Pistons' doctors.

Rather than take a chance with a highly paid player who was considered a medical question mark by the many medical sources that Houston consulted, the team would rather take its chances on healing the emotional scars with Horry and Bullard.

"We went through the process, and it couldn't be done," Tomjanovich said. "So, we go back to our old team that was pretty damn good."

Tomjanovich knows it isn't going to be an easy process.

Horry and Bullard got the news around midafternoon and were wearing Pistons' paraphernalia when they landed at Intercontinental Airport tonight. Ouch.

This thing has turned into a mess.

Did the Pistons try to pull a fast one by peddling damaged goods? Did the Rockets err by not demanding that Elliott's medical records be sent for inspection before the announcement of the trade?

It really doesn't matter now.

Horry and Bullard will be at Rockets' practice tomorrow. Maybe the club should hire Dr. Joyce Brothers to check out this group's collective psyche.

February 7

People are getting awfully jittery around here.

During today's practice at The Summit, Herrera was seen leaving the building early. Within minutes, there were rumors circulating that Herrera had been traded.

Not true. Herrera had simply gotten into a skirmish at practice with Maxwell. Tomjanovich then sent Herrera home so cooler heads could prevail.

Tomjanovich met individually with Horry and Bullard this morning. Horry was pretty low-key, but Bullard—an impending unrestricted free agent—launched a campaign for the Rockets to end this aborted trade saga by giving him a seven-figure contract extension.

Bullard said the Pistons' organization had expressed over the weekend that he would have plenty of opportunities for extended minutes, which could leave him with more bargaining leverage at the end of the year. By going back to the Rockets, Bullard reasoned, he would play less time on a better team. That was OK with Bullard as long as Alexander would take care of him financially with a contract of about $1.2 million annually.

"I'm just saying now that I'm back here, give me what I'm worth," said Bullard, who is averaging 3.9 points while averaging 12 minutes per game.

At this tenuous juncture, I seriously doubt the Rockets intend to give Matt anything.

February 8

The Rockets were a pitiful sight tonight in Milwaukee.

After sending Elliott away because of a kidney ailment, they should be concerned with the heads of those who have remained. The lowly Milwaukee Bucks spoiled the return of Horry and Bullard by whipping the listless Houstonians 106–98.

"Nothing has changed," Horry said. "I came back to the same old stuff."

Don't look now, but the team that opened the season 22–1 is just one-half game ahead of hard-charging San Antonio in the Midwest Division race. Houston has dropped five in a row on the road, and players are wondering who will be shopped next in the 15 days leading up to the trading deadline.

The good news is that we're just one game away from All-Star Weekend. These players are emotionally drained from all the crap that has been going on. They need to get away from it for awhile.

February 9

Clearly, Horry's feelings are badly bruised. I think he'll be OK in the long run because, as they say, time heals all wounds. But it's going to be touch-and-go for Robert these next few weeks.

The Rockets practiced in Milwaukee today before heading on to . . . you guessed it, Detroit. As the team was loosening up before the workout, Horry ambled over to the sideline and peeked at my computer screen.

"You've got a good job at the newspaper; they can't just ship you off to another town," Horry told me.

"Robert, you're making a guaranteed $1.2 million this year," I replied. "For $1.2 million, they could ship me off to work at a weekly in Siberia."

The aftershocks from the aborted trade just won't end.

Les Alexander arranged a teleconference from his Boca Raton, Fla., home this afternoon to refute Detroit coach Don Chaney's comment that "somebody got cold feet" when the Elliott deal was rescinded.

There was also media speculation that the Rockets pulled out of the deal because of an unwillingness to make a huge financial commitment to Elliott.

Alexander could have saved his breath because the Rockets were being vindicated even as Alexander was speaking. Elliott announced he would take an indefinite leave of absence to clear up his medical problem.

On to Detroit for more fun and frolic.

Remember the movie *Trading Places,* starring Eddie Murphy and Jamie Lee Curtis? The Rockets and Pistons can counter with Trading Places, starring Horry and Bullard.

February 10

Horry had his own movie analogy when he walked into The Palace tonight and greeted the Detroit media.

The Trade That Wasn't continued to be the central topic in this haunting setting. Horry had to dwell on it again.

"It was like *Home Alone,* where your parents leave you," Horry said.

It is becoming increasingly apparent that Horry won't be able to recommit himself to the Rockets emotionally until after the Feb. 24 trading deadline. He is convinced the team is still trying to deal him.

Despite all the shakiness, the Rockets finally got a road win tonight, mainly because the Pistons were terrible and dog tired after playing in Boston the previous evening.

Houston heads into the All-Star break 34–12. Only Seattle has a better record.

"We've been through a lot lately, but you look at our record and that's not too shabby," Tomjanovich said.

February 11

The NBA threw a big party at the Metrodome tonight for everyone attending All-Star Weekend. The food was great and the atmosphere relaxing. But alas, this Horry/Elliott saga is like a bad dream that you just can't escape.

Bruce Moseley, one of the Rockets' team physicians, came along to say he had heard from a San Antonio writer that Kinerk is trying to revive the Elliott trade talks with Les Alexander, based on an independent kidney examination that Elliott had taken earlier in the day at the University of Arizona.

Rudy later showed up at the party with his family and said he had heard nothing about a revived deal.

This doesn't make any sense. Regardless of what the Arizona doctors told Elliott, it's not going to change the opinion of the Rockets' doctors. If Elliott couldn't pass a Rockets physical last week, he can't pass it now.

So . . . pass the nachos.

February 12

Cassell and Olajuwon are representing the Rockets during All-Star Weekend. The savvy kid and the great veteran.

Cassell played in the inaugural Rookie All-Star game tonight and scored seven points in a critical two-minute flurry that helped his team win. I wasn't too sure about Cassell when the season started. In preseason, he couldn't make an outside shot. But I'm beginning to see why Rudy is so high on the kid.

He competes defensively and has a bulldog attitude and a God-given knack for penetration.

Hakeem is currently the man to beat for regular-season MVP honors, but David Robinson is moving up fast on the outside thanks to

San Antonio's torrid last month. A big All-Star game by Olajuwon tomorrow would boost national awareness that he is truly the most dominant player in the game.

All the national media heavyweights are here in Minneapolis, waiting to be impressed.

February 13

Hakeem played well, but Scottie Pippen emerged as the star of stars.

In the East's 127–118 victory over the West, Pippen scored 29 points, including five three-pointers. He was the unanimous MVP of the All-Star Game, but Olajuwon might well have been the voter's choice if the West had won. Olajuwon had 19 points, 11 rebounds and five blocks in what ranked as the best of his nine appearances in All-Star competition.

"In the beginning, I had a good chance (of an MVP award)," Olajuwon said. "But I figured my team would have to win the game."

At halftime, I spotted Les Alexander in the stands and went up to ask if he had heard from Kinerk. The Houston owner said there's no truth to the rumor about an Elliott trade being revived.

George Karl would say hurrah on that one.

Karl, who nipped Tomjanovich for the Western Conference All-Star coaching berth, had become concerned when he first read about the Rockets trading for Elliott.

"We were ticked off," Karl said. "Our feeling was that Elliott was just what that team needed. We do some things against Houston defensively that Sean might have been able to counter."

While acknowledging the Rockets would have emotional scars to deal with in bringing Horry back, Karl said he still considers Houston a viable championship contender.

"There's a little bit of a nightmare there, but every team in the league has problems," Karl said. "We're 35–10, and we still have some unhappy players. Ten years ago, winning cured all ills. Players were much more respectful of winning. In today's game, they respect winning, but they still have an opinion on 'getting mine'. I'm not sure that makes our game right. But it definitely exists. All teams have to deal with it."

February 14

This just in from Gossip Center: Word on the trading grapevine is that the Rockets have turned their attention from Elliott to Danny Manning.

The Los Angeles Clippers are in a terrible situation with Manning. If he is with the team past Feb. 24, Manning has declared he'll play out the year and sign elsewhere as an unrestricted free agent. Thus, Los Angeles must trade Manning in the next 10 days in order to salvage some type of compensation.

Manning was sitting in a Minneapolis hotel ballroom three days ago, talking about his preferred list of teams. He didn't mention the Rockets, but the player doesn't really have any control in the matter. The Clippers will dictate if he goes and where he goes.

Would the Rockets give up Thorpe and/or Horry for Manning?

It's possible, I guess. But the Rockets would have to get a guarantee that Manning would be with them beyond this season.

Here we go again. More trade intrigue.

Can't this Rockets team just leave well enough alone?

February 15

When they took the court tonight against the strong Atlanta Hawks, the Rockets looked like they were still on All-Star vacation. They wallowed around for 15 minutes, falling behind by 17 points. At that juncture, the Houston fans were probably thinking six or seven deals would be appropriate before the trading deadline.

But Houston staged a spirited comeback with Olajuwon dominating the middle and Smith outplaying All-Star Mookie Blaylock at the point. Houston's defense limited Dominique Wilkins to 9 of 25 shooting, and the Rockets walked away with a 103–99 victory.

Even a home-court victory over an Eastern Conference power wasn't enough to quiet the trade-frenzy gossip. Outside the Board Room, one of the team's peripheral voices was saying the Rockets had recently checked out Miami's Glen Rice as a possible acquisition.

I really don't know if there's anything to this. Rudy simply won't comment on trade speculation, and there's no general manager to provide an insight into the club's maneuvering.

But I do know the prevailing feeling here at Ten Greenway Plaza is that Houston doesn't have enough offense to win a championship.

People are worried that when the playoffs roll around, there won't be a definitive second option to count on once teams set their defense for Olajuwon.

Jordan had Pippen as a No. 2 accomplice with the Three-peat Bulls. Isiah Thomas had Joe Dumars as an All-Star sidekick on those Pistons' championship teams.

Apparently, the Rockets want to trade for a shooter who has plenty of snap, crackle and pop.

Right now, Rockets' types nervously figure it's Hakeem or Bust.

February 16

One baby step forward, one giant leap backward.

After the encouraging comeback win over Atlanta last night, the Rockets embarrassed themselves tonight in Charlotte by losing to an injury-wrecked Hornets team that was without Alonzo Mourning and Larry Johnson.

The Hornets came in with an eight-game losing streak and started a CBA-like front line of Marty Conlon, David Wingate and Kenny Gattison. Hard to believe the Rockets could lose a game like this, but they did.

The club just isn't competing defensively for 48 minutes anymore.

This is becoming a streaky aggregation. Last night, the Rockets got away with a lethargic start. Tonight, they spotted Charlotte a 19-point lead in the opening 14 minutes, and it cost them in the end.

The Rockets are 13–12 over the last 25 games.

Panic time, perhaps? I'll bet the trade winds will really be at hurricane force when we get home tomorrow.

February 17

The real question here is whether the Rockets are as good as the 22–1 start or as mediocre as the 13–12 record since Dec. 23 would indicate.

I called Les Alexander in Boca Raton today and asked if the team had anything cooking with a week to go before the trading deadline.

"All I can say is that we're always looking to improve the club if we can," Les said. "We were looking to improve when we were 15–0. I'm not the kind of owner who likes to sit around."

The latest scuttlebutt is that Sacramento is trying to ship small forward Lionel Simmons to Houston for Horry. And two New York outlets are reporting the Knicks have contacted Houston about Horry.

What's happening is that teams are circling the Rockets and looking to pick up a steal. Because of the Horry/Elliott trade fiasco, the league seems to believe Houston is vulnerable. Teams don't believe the Rockets will keep Horry because of the awkward aspects involved with counting on a player who had been shipped out.

You can't blame teams for trying to pick up a young, quality asset for relatively meager compensation.

Still, I can't see Rudy settling for 60 cents on the dollar. Unless he can get equal value for Horry—and that wound entail getting a player of Manning's ability—Horry has to stay.

Remember, time heals all wounds. Get Robert past the trading deadline and I'll bet he'll begin to feel like a true Rocket again.

I stopped by the office of Sally Clack late this afternoon. Sally handles administrative duties for the basketball team, and Tomjanovich's office is in the same wing.

Tomjanovich's door was closed, but as I was walking out of Sally's office, I heard Rudy screaming from the top of his lungs.

"You're (bleeping) yourself! Who's going to back these people up!"

Whew, boy. It gets more bizarre every day.

I'm with Robert Horry. Just get me past that trading deadline.

February 18

With all this trade speculation, the players are now being asked if they think Houston needs a personnel adjustment.

The judgment: No, no and no.

Talking with *The Houston Post*'s Carlton Thompson, Thorpe elaborated on the subject after today's practice, saying a trade was not the solution to the Rockets' problems.

"The solution lies within the team," the Rockets' co-captain said. "We have to realize what we have and use that to our advantage. The media can have all the rumors they want, but I really feel like if this team was doing it early in the season, we can do it now. If we don't change our attitudes, things are going to continue to be the same."

Thorpe believes it's a misconception that the Rockets don't have a viable second option on offense.

"We already have a lot of options," he said. "It's just a matter of utilizing them. We are so programmed now to run a play a certain way that we forget about all of the other options involved in that play. We've been too predictable.

"We have the personnel to win a championship, but we're not playing like a championship team. We're not focused like we were at the beginning of the season when we were playing like every game counted."

February 19

The streaking San Antonio Spurs are the talk of the league. They won again tonight for their 12th in a row and now have a one-game lead on the Rockets in the loss column.

This Midwest Division race is really going to be something. The Spurs and Rockets still have four head-to-head meetings on the schedule. It's going to come down to which team avoids significant injuries and shows the mental toughness to handle the grind of a long, long season.

The Rockets kept pace tonight by whipping a tired Phoenix club. The Suns were playing in a back-to-back situation and didn't have enough spring in their legs to stay with Houston.

Thorpe hit 9 of 9 shots and had 18 rebounds. Horry had his best offensive game in a long time, running the floor with abandon and finishing with 18 points, nine rebounds and five assists.

"I hear all about Houston's problems," Suns coach Paul Westphal said. "But I sure didn't see any out there tonight."

February 20

Ron Grinker, the Cincinnati-based agent for Danny Manning, returned my phone call today.

Grinker confirmed he had talked with Rockets officials on an exploratory basis concerning a Manning trade. Grinker said it was etched in stone that Manning would not guarantee any team trading for him and that he would continue with that organization beyond this year.

"The team that trades for Danny will have to be confident it can make Danny want to continue to be part of that organization," Grinker said.

When I suggested it would be an extremely risky proposition to give up one or two nucleus players for a guy who wasn't locked in beyond this year, Grinker pointed out that getting a Manning might be the difference in putting a team over the top for a championship.

"If Jerry Colangelo of Phoenix were in a salary-cap position to do a deal with the Clippers, I'm sure he would come after Danny," Grinker said. "Jerry is a very aggressive guy, and he wants a championship."

The Rockets want a championship, too.

But I just can't see them breaking up a 36–13 nucleus unless they have a guarantee that Manning will be a Rocket for at least five years.

February 22

Olajuwon and Denver guard Mahmoud Abdul-Rauf are observing Ramadan, the Muslim holy month that began Feb. 11. Followers fast from sunrise to sunset each day.

Before tonight's Rockets victory over the Nuggets, Olajuwon said he and Abdul-Rauf would break the fast together. The two have become close, with their devout Muslim beliefs serving as the common bond.

"Once you are brothers, there is love right there," Olajuwon said.

It strikes me that Hakeem's ascension to Most Valuable Player consideration parallels his ascension to Most Valuable Person. There is no doubt his spiritual awakening a couple of years ago has enabled him to blossom into a mature, compassionate man.

Hakeem's dream year on the court is reinforcing the notion that good things happen to good people.

At the age of 31, this is a man who has it all together.

February 23

Everybody is eager to find out who will win the Manning Sweepstakes. We'll know by 8 p.m. tomorrow.

The hottest rumor has Manning going to Atlanta for Dominique Wilkins. The deal would work from a salary-cap standpoint. Wilkins is going to be an unrestricted free agent at the end of the year, and the Hawks don't believe they'll have any better chance of signing him than Manning, a younger and overall better player.

But the word around the league is that clubs such as Portland, Miami and Houston are still talking to the Clippers about contingency proposals. If the Rockets were to trade for Manning and then not be able to re-sign him at the end of the year, for example, maybe the Clippers would kick in a contingency No. 1 draft pick.

One way or the other, the championship picture is going to be altered by what happens in these next 24 hours.

February 24

The big news came in the midst of the Rockets-Knicks game. The Wilkins-Manning deal went through, and the Hawks are being trumpeted as a championship-caliber team.

For the Rockets, the net result of a full month's trade commotion has been no change in the rotation.

For better or worse, Horry is staying. For better or worse, the Rockets will try to win a championship with the same basic group which had reported to Galveston on Oct. 7.

The Rockets drubbed the Knicks 93–73 tonight, and Tomjanovich seemed to be more relaxed than I'd seen him in a month.

Until, that is, somebody mentioned during the postgame news conference that another trade that had gone down. Minutes before the deadline, Philadelphia shipped sharpshooter Jeff Hornacek to Utah for Jeff Malone.

"What!" Tomjanovich shouted.

February 26

It appears the two-team race in the Midwest Division is going to escalate into a three-team race. The Utah Jazz has been rejuvenated by the Hornacek trade. With Hornacek making his Utah debut tonight at The Summit, the Jazz downed the Rockets 95–85.

Jeff Malone is a darn good player but lacks the range of a Hornacek. With Karl Malone demanding double-team attention in the post, Hornacek should be able to give Utah better court spacing.

"Their chemistry is going to change drastically because Hornacek can spread the floor," Tomjanovich said. "I think he's one of the best shooting guards in the league. That's no disrespect to Jeff Malone because he was a Rocket-killer, too."

Utah insiders think Karl Malone spurred the Jazz organization into pushing for a deal. Malone had said during All-Star Weekend he didn't want to continue playing for the Jazz if the organization wasn't committed to winning a title.

Malone seems delighted with the trade and so do his teammates. This means the Rockets and Spurs have to be looking back with some degree of trepidation.

The Rockets kept dialing from long distance tonight, but 19 of their 22 attempts from three-point range went astray.

Who's this intruder at the Rockets-Spurs party? Somebody needs to inform the Jazz that two's company and three's a crowd.

February 28

A couple of months ago, the Rockets were inventing ways to win the close games. They've lost the copyright.

In a rematch against the Jazz at the Delta Center, Houston again shot itself out of the game by missing 17 of 20 three-pointers. The perimeter ineptitude was a critical factor in a 89–85 loss.

For those who are counting, that's seven losses in the last eight Rockets road games. Houston finished February just 7–5, and March won't be any better unless the three-point shooters get hot.

"We either have to start hitting the threes or stop taking them," Tomjanovich said. "You have to fold a losing hand."

Tough month.

I'll bet the Rockets are happy to flip the page on their calendar.

March 1

For a month, the Rockets searched outside the organization for someone who could bring another dimension to the Houston offense.

Could it be they've now found a new dimension within the cozy confines of their own family?

Cassell was the man tonight in a victory over Orlando. He kept driving . . . and driving . . . and driving. The rookie scored 14 consecutive points in the second half, and that show of penetration magic gave Tomjanovich and the Rockets plenty to think about.

"Sam's my new hero," Olajuwon said.

For much of the season, the Rockets have gotten by primarily with post-up power and the outside spot shots. The outside shots haven't been going lately, which means penetration is a necessity. Smith has been reluctant to attack off the dribble, so Cassell's banner showing against Orlando could reopen a quarterback controversy.

"This team needs to drive more," Cassell said. "We've been settling too much for the three-pointer."

Tomjanovich said after the game Cassell deserves more playing time.

That only leaves one question: How will Rudy slice the point-guard pie?

March 3

The big decisions keep on coming for Rudy T. In the wake of Cassell's penetration-fest against the Magic the other night, the Smith-bashers are out in earnest. A lot of the armchair coaches are calling Tomjanovich's KTRH radio show and recommending Cassell be promoted to starting point guard.

It's the "everybody loves the backup quarterback" syndrome.

Tomjanovich said today after practice he is indeed contemplating a changing of the guards for Saturday's game against the Clippers.

"I'm going to hold off until Friday or just before the game Saturday," Tomjanovich said. "It's something where I have a couple of days to look at the situations. I value jobs and roles. Being an ex-player, I hold them in high regard.

"If I did make a change, it would be by putting a lot of thought into it. I'm not a guy who just comes out on a whim and just changes things around."

I like Cassell and believe he's going to be a fine point guard in this league. But to start him now would be a gross overreaction.

Like it or not, the bottom line is that the Rockets aren't going to reach their full potential in the playoffs unless Smith is a part of the offensive equation. He was the team's No. 2 playoff scorer last year, averaging 14.8 points on .492 shooting. Ditch Smith now and you probably shatter his confidence and lose him completely.

Maybe it's time for those radio callers to start loving Smith for what he can do, rather than hating him for what he can't do.

Remember, it's the sum of the parts that counts.

March 4

After careful contemplation, Rudy has made his decision: Smith remains in the starting lineup.

Cassell? He's getting a promotion. Instead of spot duty, he'll play consistent minutes as a member of the basic bench rotation. This decision will either 1) squeeze Brooks' minutes at the point or 2) squeeze minutes from front-line players if Elie spends a lot of time at small forward rather than big guard.

"My feeling is that we should add to the mix instead of change the mix," Tomjanovich said after today's practice. We've gotten where we are by being a chemistry team over the years.

"I'm going with the same starting lineup, but Sam deserves to play."

Smith admitted today he was disappointed that Tomjanovich had even mentioned to the media there might be a change in the starting lineup.

"I thought the comments (by Tomjanovich) fed into it and conjured up controversy rather than team unity," Smith said. "I just feel we should be conjuring up unity . . .

"Right now, I feel real comfortable about the rest of the season. I feel at peace with myself. I've gotten everything off my chest, and everybody knows what I'm thinking."

March 5

The revised point-guard rotation looked great tonight. Smith shook off the mini-controversy by hitting 10 of 13 shots. Cassell was 3 of 6 from the floor in 14 minutes, and Brooks hit 4 of 5 shots in 14 minutes.

There's a qualifier, however.

The Rockets were playing a Clippers team that failed to put forth a professional defensive effort. Wilkins is the team's marquee attraction now, and it's evident his only concern is scoring as many points as he can and jacking up his impending free-agency market value. This Los Angeles bunch is a sad, selfish, terrible team.

Considering that Houston must play San Antonio, Seattle and San Antonio again next week, I wonder if this .582 shooting performance against the Clippers' non-defense will lull the Rockets into a false sense of security.

The 40–15 Rockets might have found better competition at the downtown YMCA.

March 6

We're starting to get down to the nitty-gritty in this MVP debate. Olajuwon and Robinson are both having great years, and I figure it's only fair that the man who leads his team to the Midwest Division title should get the award.

The Bulls are stumbling now, so Pippen has probably fallen back in the MVP race. With the Rockets and Spurs about to play each other twice in a five-day span, there's an individual subplot to go with the team plot.

"I'm not into the politics that go along with these awards," Robinson said. "I'm just about winning. If my team wins, then I think the award situation will take care of itself."

One way or the other, the MVP is going to be a Texas center.

Who says this is a football state?

March 8

The Rockets should have their rallying cry for the final 26 games of the regular season: Remember the Alamodome.

In what was supposed to be the biggest game of the year, Houston played as though it was the exhibition opener. The Spurs took it 115–99, and it wasn't nearly as close as the final score indicated.

No fire, no chance. Suddenly, it's the *second-place* Rockets.

The Spurs, who took a one-game lead in the division, simply drove the Rockets to the ground and rubbed their noses in the dirt. The Spurs did everything well from a basketball standpoint and still had enough energy left to taunt Houston unmercifully.

"I'm very disappointed," Tomjanovich said. "We've been so competitive in the big games, but we just didn't match their intensity tonight."

I'm thinking about that bold statement made by Spurs guard Sleepy Floyd in preseason. His prediction that San Antonio would "definitely" win the division seemed absurb when Houston jumped out 22–1.

But now the 43–17 Spurs lead the 40–16 Rockets.

Still a long way to go, however.

The Rockets may yet wind up with the last laugh if they ever find second gear.

March 9

Here's a rather sobering thought for Rockets' fans: After a 15–0 getaway, Houston isn't even assured of having a home-court advantage in the first round of the playoffs.

As I look at the Western Conference rankings in the morning paper, I see that the Jazz has won 10 in a row to pull within one-half game of the second-place Rockets.

For the sake of argument, let's assume Houston finishes below both the Spurs and Jazz. Let's further assume the Rockets stay behind 43–14 Seattle.

Houston would have to finish ahead of Phoenix for a first-round home-court edge. The Suns trail Houston by 3½ games but certainly have the potential to run off a big streak.

Attention, Rockets.

Better get busy.

March 10

George Karl just can't stand these visits to The Summit.

Each time he comes into this building, the Sonics' coach gets knocked off his high horse. The Rockets shut down Seattle's offense again tonight, holding the Sonics to .352 shooting. Houston won 87–82, and there was a dispute about whether the Rockets' defense defused the Sonics or the Sonics defused themselves.

Tomjanovich thought his team played great defense. Karl said it was more a case of the Sonics having a poor offensive night.

"We miss shots in this building we ordinarily make," Karl said.

Clearly, Karl doesn't want Houston to get any type of psychological edge. He wants his team to believe it can beat the Rockets anytime. There's a strong possibility these teams could meet in the Western Conference Finals, and Karl really wanted tonight's game because a victory would have given the Sonics positive reinforcement they could win in Houston during the playoffs.

The Sonics dropped all three playoff games in Houston last year. They finished 0–2 at The Summit this season. To them, The Summit is a Chamber of Horrors.

Seattle had an early 14-point cushion but shot only 29 percent in the second half. Even though Olajuwon missed 7:20 in the second half because of foul trouble, the Sonics couldn't put Houston away.

That's the big picture.

And here's the little picture: With Smith and Cassell playing regular minutes at the point, Brooks has begun to feel the point-guard squeeze. The smallest Rocket did not play against Seattle, and that could be a sign of the future.

"My jersey says 'Brooks' on the back and 'Rockets' on the front," Brooks said after the game. "The team is always more important than the individual."

It's hard for me to imagine a Rockets' rotation without the spunky Brooks, but it looks like that's where the club is headed.

When you've got three competent point guards, somebody has to sit.

March 11

There's no time for the Rockets to savor last night's win. They're already thinking about getting revenge for the horror show in San Antonio earlier this week.

The Spurs not only beat the Rockets, they humiliated the Rockets.

There was Willie Anderson, yapping incessantly at Smith while following Smith into the Rockets' huddle with the Spurs up by 17.

There was Dennis Rodman, gesturing at the Rockets' bench with San Antonio up by 24. There was Rodman again, strutting proudly off the floor with arms held high after his ejection for taunting.

At times, it had been hard to tell whether the Spurs were into basketball or pro wrestling theatrics.

"We felt like they taunted us and showed us up," Maxwell said. "I felt a lot of it was unnecessary. They had us down, and they were showing us up. So, I guess we need to upgrade our enthusiasm."

Translation: The Rockets intend to meet force with force tomorrow night. Mad Max usually sets the tone when an emotional upgrade is required.

"My 11 teammates will be wild and crazy," Maxwell said with a smile. "Me, I'll be calm."

Sure, Max, sure.

March 12

The Spurs are operating on Central Time. Dennis Rodman is operating on Rodman Time.

The controversial forward walked into The Summit for tonight's 7:30 game at 7:17. He had missed the team flight from San Antonio, and Coach John Lucas disciplined Rodman by holding him out of the game.

Rodman wrote a magic-marker message on a towel and held it up throughout the game for the fans and the television cameras: "I'm Sorry. Can I Play Now!"

As it turned out, Lucas didn't need Rodman. For the second time in a week, the Rockets started Thorpe defensively on Robinson, hoping that strategy would keep Olajuwon out of foul trouble.

But that ploy backfired. Robinson got in a rhythm early against Thorpe and Olajuwon got into foul trouble anyway while trying to go out on the floor and guard J.R. Reid. Furthermore, the Rockets were burned when they double-teamed Robinson because the San Antonio center was able to kick the ball out for easy spot shots.

Robinson finished with 40 points, 16 rebounds, seven assists and five blocks. He may now have the edge over Olajuwon in the MVP race, since the Spurs are in first place by one-half game.

"There's your MVP," Lucas said emphatically while commenting on Robinson's monster game.

For one night, at least, it was hard to argue the point.

But when these teams play again, look for Olajuwon to guard Robinson straight-up. A different strategy could mean a different result.

March 14

There are no automatic wins in the NBA. But a trip to Dallas is the closest thing to it.

The Rockets picked up their obligatory victory at Reunion Arena last night, and the most noteworthy statistic was Maxwell's 27 points. Maybe that rampage will bring Vernon out of a long winter's shooting slump.

In his opening 23 games, Maxwell shot .434 from the field and an attractive .379 from three-point range. Over his next 34 games, he shot just .340 from the floor, with a polar-like .214 percentage from three-point range.

Hakeem said he had a talk with Vernon recently, reinforcing how important Maxwell is to this ballclub. Maybe that pep talk did some good.

March 15

On game days at home, the Rockets generally have a shootaround from 11 a.m. to about noon or 12:15. They shower, head home for a leisurely afternoon and then return to the arena around 6 p.m.

I saw Vernon in the locker room after today's shootaround. It must have been around 12:45. Two hours later, the office called to inform me that Maxwell had been arrested for the third time in the last two years by the Houston Police Department. There had been an incident in which Maxwell was alleged to have waved a gun at a man in the parking lot of a Luby's Cafeteria on Buffalo Speedway. Maxwell was being charged with illegally carrying a weapon, a Class A misdemeanor.

It's always something. I take my eyes off these guys for a couple of hours and look what happens.

Vernon was released after roughly a six-hour stint at police headquarters. He showed up at The Summit just before halftime and wound up playing the entire second half against Portland. Houston rallied from a 10-point deficit heading into the final period and won 105–99.

Maxwell apologized to his teammates when they came in for the halftime break trailing by nine. The distracted, disoriented Rockets accepted the apology and then kicked some butt in the second half.

"He said he was sorry for missing the first half, and that's enough for us," Smith said. "The biggest thing is that he knows he let us down. We didn't have any focus in the first half.

"But people make mistakes all the time. Athletes are no different."

March 16

It looks like everything is going to settle down following the Maxwell arrest. Vernon had to appear in court this morning and a March 24 arraignment was set. Maxwell made it back to The Summit for practice. He denied pointing a gun at anyone and later explained why he was carrying a .380 semiautomatic pistol in the front seat of his car.

Maxwell said the gun was for his safety.

"It's a law you shouldn't be riding with a pistol in your car," Maxwell said. "I had one in mine, and I got burned. I got caught. But I'll bet 80 percent of Houston rides with pistols in their cars because the crime rate around here is crazy. It's for protection.

"Something almost happened to me once before, and I said I'd never let it happen again. I feel bad for my family. It's embarrassing. But I'm sure a lot of people realize and understand me.

"I'm a high-profile guy. If a situation were to arise, I'd want to be well taken care of. I don't want to be left in a situation I can't handle. I want to take care of myself.

"I feel like you should be able to carry a pistol instead of a rifle. They say you can ride with a rifle in your front seat. I don't understand it."

The 43–17 Rockets can ill afford major distractions if they hope to win this ultra-competitive division. The Spurs are focused. The Jazz is focused. Houston had better be focused, too.

Asked how the Maxwell situation would affect the team as it prepares for the stretch run, Tomjanovich said: "I think we're just going to move on from here."

March 19

Les Alexander wants a new home for the Rockets. He claims the ballclub can't survive economically in The Summit and has been working in conjunction with Oilers owner Bud Adams in hopes of building a downtown domed stadium for basketball and football.

But the project hasn't received much positive public support, and an Alexander acquaintance said before tonight's Pistons-Rockets game that Alexander believes the domed stadium project is dead.

"Is it dead?" I asked Les.

"Probably," he said.

Plan B would call for Alexander to build his own basketball-only facility, preferably at a downtown site. But talking about it conceptually and getting it built and paid for are two different things.

Meanwhile, the people who run The Summit are bewildered by Alexander. They can't understand why he won't throw his support behind a proposed $30 million improvement project for the existing arena.

This figures to be a nasty, protracted, backroom fight with heavy economic and political implications.

What's happening on the court is a lot more exciting.

March 20

Elie had a career game last night in the Rockets' victory over the Pistons.

He hit 9 of 9 shots, including a trio of three-pointers. He also had a career-high 15 rebounds as Houston prevailed 106–88 to take a one-half game lead in the Midwest race.

Elie's performance reminded me he'll be an unrestricted free agent at the end of the season. Since the Rockets still don't have a vice president of basketball operations, Les Alexander has been serving as the point man in contract negotiations. Elie has been offered a four-year deal for $6 million, but he wants to wait and see how things shake out the remainder of the season.

It's a calculated gamble.

If Elie performs well and the Rockets go deep into the playoffs, Elie's market value will be greatly enhanced.

But if the Rockets crater or Elie suffers a serious injury, he might wish he had taken the instant security.

I like the idea of a player waiting until the off-season to handle contract matters. Do the job first and then ask for your raise.

That's the way it works in real life, isn't it?

March 21

Kenny Smith looks 10 years younger.

The Rockets point guard lost a bet over the weekend when his beloved alma mater, North Carolina, was upset 75–72 by Boston College in the NCAA Tournament. Smith had said if the Tar Heels lost, he would shave off his mustache.

Razor, please.

"I'll definitely make a call to (North Carolina coach) Dean Smith," Smith said.

Smith is feeling strange without the mustache.

"It seems like it has been there forever," Smith said.

Relax, Kenny. By this time next week, the mustache will be back.

March 22

The news flash came in the midst of tonight's Rockets game at Minnesota. A Los Angeles radio station was reporting Magic Johnson would be replacing embattled Randy Pfund as the interim Lakers head coach.

By the time Elie's make-or-break shot hit the back rim and bounced long, preserving Minnesota's 83–81 victory, the story on Johnson had been confirmed.

The revelation that Magic was venturing into the coaching ranks overshadowed the Houston road loss. The Lakers are coming to Houston on Thursday, and everybody in the Rockets' locker room was wondering if Johnson would make his coaching debut at The Summit.

"I think he'll be a good coach," Olajuwon said. "He knows how to get the job done. The Lakers' players will be pumped up. They'll be trying to impress Magic."

Added Brooks: "It's like a new life for those guys. Magic will have all the players' respect. If you can't respect Magic, you shouldn't be playing this game. Who wouldn't want to run through a brick wall for Magic? He was the NBA."

From a Rockets angle, this Johnson development could indeed become significant. Houston has two games against the Lakers in the next 10 days. If the Lakers are playing with a surge of adrenaline because of the coaching change, it just might make the difference in the Midwest Division race.

The Rockets don't care to play any team right now that has a Magic touch.

March 24

Magic wasn't here. After some initial confusion leading to conflicting news reports, Johnson has decided to make his coaching debut at The Forum Sunday against Milwaukee.

Assistant Bill Bertka was in charge of the Lakers' bench tonight while Johnson was watching on television from the Los Angeles area. Johnson had to like the Lakers' effort. But Olajuwon was just too much.

The relentless Olajuwon scored 25 of his 37 points in the second half, and the Rockets rode the big man's shoulders to a 113–107 victory.

The Dream was coming off a 10-of-27 shooting performance in Minnesota. That's the common denominator of the superstars: They seldom have two subpar games in a row.

"I was a player in this league, and I know how hard it is to make big plays," Tomjanovich said. "Hakeem? He makes big play after big play after big play."

The Rockets have seesawed a game ahead of the Spurs with 17 to go.

But after Saturday's home game against Utah, the Rockets have to leave for a five-game Western swing, their longest road trip of the year.

Looks like that trip will go a long way in deciding the Midwest champ.

March 26

The Rockets picked up the getaway game against Utah and then headed for Hobby Airport for the late-night flight to Phoenix.

Going into this five-game trip, it looks as though Rudy has set his basic eight-man rotation for the key juncture of the season. It's the same starting five, with Elie, Herrera and Cassell off the bench.

Brooks didn't play again tonight. It looks like his role from now on will be making the nucleus players better in practice and leading the cheers from the sideline.

I feel bad for Scott because he didn't play his way out of the rotation. It was more a case of Cassell seizing the opportunity and playing his way *into* the rotation.

Rudy is taking a chance here. The rookie is good, but who knows how a rookie is going to react under playoff pressure? Brooks has playoff experience and gives it everything he has got. Maybe the Rockets just believe they need a bigger, stronger guard to go to the conference finals and beyond.

On the plane ride to Phoenix, I'm thinking about Cassell and how he'll respond down the stretch and in the playoffs.

This rookie could wind up making the coach look like a genius. But if Cassell fails, the second-guessers will be asking one question:

Where's Brooks?

March 27

The biggest road trip of the year has started with double trouble.

The Rockets were blown out by the Suns 113–98 tonight, but that wasn't the worst news. Midway through the fourth quarter, Olajuwon was ejected for making contact with Official Bill Spooner. Supervisor of officials Darrel Garretson happened to be in attendance and told Rockets officials he figured Olajuwon's action would result in a one-game suspension.

With Houston trailing 88–78, Olajuwon was swarmed by three Phoenix defenders after accepting a pass. Olajuwon went to the floor, the ball was stolen and the Suns raced the other way.

As Spooner ran by, Olajuwon—from a prone position—reached out and made contact with the official.

Olajuwon's face had an incredulous expression when it was suggested after the game he might be in for a suspension.

"I was just trying to get his attention," Olajuwon said. "I touched him as he was going by, but it wasn't something I should have been ejected for. Sometimes, the refs get so sensitive."

The Rockets were a forlorn group as they left America West Arena. They know it's likely they'll have to play Sacramento on Tuesday without Olajuwon.

For Houston, this trip must already seem like a journey to nowhere.

March 28

When I called NBA Operations Chief Rod Thorn this morning about the Olajuwon situation, he told me to check one succinct paragraph in the NBA rulebook:

"Any player or coach guilty of intentional physical contact with an official shall automatically be suspended without pay for one game. A fine and/or longer period of suspension will result if circumstances dictate."

Case closed.

Olajuwon received the news of the suspension en route to the Phoenix airport. As he awaited the team's flight to Sacramento, Olajuwon told me this suspension could turn out to be a blessing in disguise.

For three months, the Rockets have been groping to find their early-season magic. Olajuwon has kept them near the top of the Western Conference standings, but the supporting cast will have to blossom for Houston to stay afloat in the latter rounds of the playoffs.

This could be a chance for players to gain confidence in their own skills rather than depending on Olajuwon.

"Everybody can raise their game to another level," Olajuwon suggested. "There will be more room in the middle if I'm not playing."

The way I see it, tomorrow represents a crossroads game.

If Olajuwon's theory holds true, it could be a springboard to the division title. But if the Olajuwon absence results in a Houston loss to the worst team in the conference, the Rockets may not mentally recover.

March 29

I can't ever remember a team's fortunes changing so dramatically from the first half to the second half.

The Rockets appeared to be a team out of control before intermission. Olajuwon was back at the hotel, forbidden from even entering Arco Arena. It got even worse when Herrera was ejected for throwing a punch and Maxwell was tossed for arguing an official's call. The Kings led by five at the half, and Houston was without three nucleus players.

I passed by the Rockets' quarters at halftime. Tomjanovich always stands outside the locker room for a couple of minutes, conferring with his assistants before addressing the team. His face was as red as a Rockets' road warmup jacket.

I'm not sure what Rudy said at halftime. But it must have been something Knute Rockne would have been proud of.

The Rockets exploded for 74 points in the second half, and it was like a symbolic thawing of a long winter's freeze.

This was vintage Rockets basketball. The ball was hopping, the defense was sound, the shooting was crisp, the fire was there.

Tomjanovich apparently tore into the Rockets at halftime about the siege of ejections.

"I won't have that," Tomjanovich said. "We're going to show professional behavior on the court."

Said one player: "It was the first time I'd ever really heard Rudy raise his voice."

Remember this victory. We may look back on it as a turning point.

March 30

The news hadn't been all good in Sacramento. Elie was hit on the hand by Sacramento's LaBradford Smith, and the Rockets learned before tonight's game against the Warriors that Elie will be sidelined three to four weeks.

The fourth metacarpal in Elie's right hand is fractured and may require a surgical procedure. Elie is really down about it, but the doctors are telling him he could return by the start of the playoffs.

This means Maxwell, Smith and Cassell have to carry the load at the guard spots. That trio certainly did the job tonight. Maxwell had 28 points, Smith 25 and Cassell 13.

The 114–104 conquest of Golden State was Houston's first road win over a plus-.500 team since Dec. 21 in San Antonio.

"It seems like we're playing with confidence and fire again," Tomjanovich said, leaning against a wall outside the Rockets' locker room. "For the second night in a row, we had great performances from a lot of people."

What a difference it makes when both Rockets starting guards are shooting well. The defense doesn't know whether to pack it in against Olajuwon or honor the perimeter threats.

Thorpe had 18 points and 21 rebounds tonight, and Horry hit 5 of 9 shots and added eight assists.

And, oh yes, that guy named Olajuwon was back in the lineup. Remember him?

March 31

Hard to believe the Rockets have gone this deep into the season without making one roster change. That's likely to change today, however, because of Elie's projected one-month absence.

Before the flight from Oakland to Los Angeles this morning, Tomjanovich told me scout Joe Ash was scouring the CBA talent. There would be consultation regarding top candidates later in the day and the club might make a decision by early evening.

"If you decide on a player, would you give me a call?" I asked Tomjanovich.

"Sure will," he said.

Tonight, I had a telephone voice-mail message from Rudy. He said the Rockets have decided to bring in 6-4 guard Larry Robinson on a 10-day contract.

It isn't earth-shaking news. But it is a tip-off on Tomjanovich's personality. A lot of coaches wouldn't bother to call a reporter with information that most people would consider trivial. But Tomjanovich said he would and so he did.

This is truly a man of his word. I respect that.

CHAPTER FOUR

Dreamtime: April–June

A lot of Houston sports fans are intrigued by Gene Peterson, who has been the passionate voice of the Rockets for 19 years. People often ask me what kind of guy Gene *really* is, since I've traveled the skyways with him for the last 15 years.

What you hear is pretty much what you get with "Geno." He bleeds Rocket red and lists God, family and the Rockets as his priorities in life.

I have to believe golf would be No. 4 on the list.

Since recovering from a heart attack and bypass surgery last year, Gene has been back on the links in earnest, along with his radio sidekick, Jim Foley. But this has been a tough trip for Gene in terms of enjoying his time on the West Coast fairways.

He left home with a nagging sty problem that resulted in swelling above and below his left eye. Yesterday, while playing golf at Mountaingate in the Los Angeles area, his left hand was struck by somebody's errant drive, resulting in a broken third metacarpal. So, Geno showed up for tonight's Lakers-Rockets game at The Forum with a bandaged hand and a swollen left eye.

"The Voice . . . The Eye . . . The Hand," a smiling Foley bellowed.

As Gene and I taped a radio segment tonight, there was more trouble in the offing. We were sitting courtside and a basketball came zipping at us, hitting Gene smack on the broken hand.

Poor guy. How much pain can one man take?

"At least I can still talk," Peterson said weakly.

To Rockets' fans, that's all that matters.

April 2

Tomorrow is Easter Sunday and the Rockets had better not lay an egg.

Last night, the Magic factor knocked Houston off course in its bid to repeat as Midwest Division champs. The Lakers haven't lost since Magic Johnson took over on the sideline, and their defensive intensity was the difference in a 101–88 Los Angeles victory.

"If you didn't know the standings, you would have thought they were the ones playing for first place and we were the ones struggling," Tomjanovich said.

There isn't much margin for error now. Houston, 50–20, trails the 52–20 Spurs by a game. Houston desperately needs to end this trip 3–2 with a victory over the Clippers tomorrow. There's going to be a huge showdown against the Spurs next week, and the Rockets have to maintain contact in the standings before that nationally televised game rolls around.

Based on last night's lethargy, I have to wonder if the players are fully grasping how important it is to win the division.

The team that finishes second in the Midwest likely will have the home-court advantage in the playoffs through only one round. The team that wins the Midwest probably will have the home court through two rounds. That's a big difference if you're thinking about playing until June.

With 12 games remaining, we're down to the regular-season moments of truth.

April 3

Who's going to blink first, Houston or San Antonio?

The Rockets got it done today against the Clippers. Houston rolled up a 20-point halftime lead and held on 106–98 to end the five-game trip on a sweet note. My basic thought is that the Rockets easily could have disintegrated on this trip. But they hung tough with the short-handed victory in Sacramento, the hot-shooting performance at Golden State and the workmanlike effort against the Clippers.

"I still feel like we're going to win (the division)," Maxwell said. "We just have to keep getting after people defensively like we did today. I've said it all year: When we compete defensively, we're tough to beat. When we don't, we're just an average ballclub."

I'd say it's a 50–50 proposition now. If the Rockets can beat San Antonio twice, they will have a good chance of taking the division since the Jazz has fallen well off the pace after its early charge with Hornacek.

This trip was a survival test, and the Rockets passed.

Happy Easter.

April 5

I'm sitting at home tonight watching the Astros on Home Sports Entertainment. Bill Worrell, the sportscaster for all seasons, has turned in his basketball microphone for a baseball microphone.

Late in the game, Worrell passes on a rather startling basketball score: The Warriors have upset the Spurs 106–101 at the Alamodome. Without having to move from their living rooms, the Rockets are back in first place by percentage points.

Everybody around Rockets headquarters has been projecting the race to the finish line, and nobody that I know of had Golden State winning in San Antonio.

This was a major break for Houston. Now it's up to the Rockets to capitalize.

April 7

The Rockets were a sight to behold tonight against the Warriors. Having had three days off to rest its legs, Houston put together the total offensive package in a 134–102 victory.

Everybody played, everybody scored for the red-hot Rockets. They made it look as easy as throwing nickels in the ocean. The shooting fever spread from Thorpe to Horry to Olajuwon and then Smith, Cassell, Maxwell and Herrera got into the act.

This was a statement game. If the playoffs opened today, the Rockets would meet the Warriors.

"They are a better team than we are," Warriors Coach Don Nelson said, "probably a lot better."

In retrospect, maybe the Rockets should have saved some of that ammunition for Saturday's crucial matchup against the Spurs.

"I don't think I'll have to say a word to the team about that game," Tomjanovich said. "We all know what it means."

April 8

There's a playoff atmosphere in the The Summit today. The NBC-TV trucks have rolled in, and everybody is ready for a game that has daily double implications.

Tomorrow's Houston-San Antonio winner takes the inside track toward a division title with a likely Most Valuable Player on its roster. The loser will be, at least temporarily, whisked from the national spotlight.

Bill Walton, the Hall of Fame center and outspoken NBC telecaster, has been selected to work tomorrow's game. After Walton finished taping an interview with Olajuwon this afternoon, I asked the Redhead for his MVP choice.

"That's going to be decided in this game," Walton said matter-of-factly. "It's a game where all the voters will be tuned in. I'm looking forward to an unbelievably great battle."

I suggested that maybe it's a bit shallow to think an MVP could be selected based on one defining game.

"That's the way championships are often won," Walton insisted. "That's what I love about it. It comes down to that one special moment, and that's where you see great champions come forward with great games."

Media members voting for the MVP award have received their ballots within the past week. The deadline for returning those ballots to NBA headquarters is April 22.

"The MVP race is exactly like the championship race," Walton said. "It's up for grabs. Rudy doesn't lobby for Hakeem, which I respect. He lets Hakeem's playing do the talking, whereas Pat Riley (Pat Ewing's chief campaigner) and John Lucas are constantly lobbying in the media.

"You do your playing on the court, but we are in a media age," Walton went on. "I just think what happens in this game has a huge impact."

Rockets versus Spurs. Olajuwon versus Robinson. National TV. I can't wait.

April 9

Pro basketball fans along Interstate 10 had a very enlightening day.

They found out 1) the Rockets have a stronger will to win than the Spurs and 2) Olajuwon is in the driver's seat for the MVP award.

Houston was rock-solid in its 100–89 victory. The Rockets set the defensive tone early as the Spurs missed 14 of their opening 17 shots and committed six turnovers.

Oops, there it is.

Suddenly, the Rockets have a two-game lead in the division race with nine to go.

"It ain't over," Maxwell said. "But I like our position a lot better than theirs. And if we win the division, Hakeem definitely has to be MVP."

The Rockets made a defensive adjustment that probably won the game.

Olajuwon asked Tomjanovich for the opportunity to guard Robinson straight-up and that move was instrumental in Houston's surge to a 20–9 lead after one quarter. The Spurs were struggling with their outside game because Dale Ellis had a sore foot and couldn't get proper liftoff for his jumper.

Houston's perimeter troops, meanwhile, were sensational. Maxwell scored 27 points and Smith added 22.

"It was a playoff-type atmosphere, and the defense was awesome," Tomjanovich said. "The key was that our perimeter people responded by hitting the big shots."

Robinson finished with 30 points, but many of them came late, with the Spurs in a catch-up mode. Although the Admiral outscored Olajuwon 30–20, the rest of the box score indicated an overall statistical draw.

Olajuwon led 13–12 in rebounding, 7–2 in assists and 2–0 in blocks. Robinson had eight turnovers to just one for Olajuwon.

"People who didn't see the game and just pick up the box score may look at the scoring totals and conclude he won the battle," Olajuwon said. "I don't even care about that. If he won the battle, I won the war."

In the eyes of the MVP voters, that's what counts.

April 10

The Rockets are like a classy thoroughbred headed for the wire. They can smell the victory, and it looks like Tomjanovich won't even have to reach for the whip.

Houston had every reason to wave the flag of surrender tonight in Denver. Coming off the emotional victory over San Antonio and playing back-to-back in the high altitude, a loss would have been understandable even to the harshest critics.

It was going that way for 31 minutes. The Nuggets led 66–49 and seemed to be en route to an easy victory. But in early April, the Rockets have rediscovered their November and December form.

Cassell gave the team a jump-start with some excellent penetration, and Houston rallied to claim a 93–92 victory. It came down to a do-or-die possession with the Nuggets up by one. Cassell beat his man on the dribble, drew Dikembe Mutombo to him and delivered a pass to a wide-open Olajuwon for a game-winning jumper with five seconds remaining.

The assist was even more scintillating than the clutch shot.

With only a split second to react and a leading contender for Defensive Player of the Year in his path, Cassell made a pressurized play that rookies aren't supposed to make.

"It's creativity and it takes a special talent," Tomjanovich said.

This one was huge—almost as important as the victory over San Antonio on Saturday. The Spurs had been counting on Houston losing in Denver.

"San Antonio has to be crushed by this," Maxwell said.

The 54–20 Rockets are 2½ up on San Antonio with eight to play. There's even an outside chance they could catch Seattle for the No. 1 playoff seed.

The Rockets prevailed despite shooting just .357 from the field.

"Looking at the stats, it doesn't seem possible we could have won," said Olajuwon, as he reclined on the trainer's table.

This is just like the early-season joy ride.

Once again, the impossible is possible.

April 11

On the flight home from Denver, I reached a simple conclusion. If the Rockets guards continue to shoot like they have in the past 10 days, this team will play until late May or June.

But what if Smith goes back into a shell, Maxwell reverts to his icy ways of January and February and Cassell gets rookie-itis?

That's how fragile this thing is.

Right now, Houston's three-guard rotation reminds me of 1991 when Smith, Maxwell and Sleepy Floyd got on a roll and helped Houston run off a 29–5 streak.

"Yeah, it's real similar," Maxwell said. "All three guys are quick and can play either guard position. We're sort of interchangeable out there, which provides a lot of options. If two of the three guards are having a good night, we've got a real good shot at winning the ballgame."

With the three-guard rotation thriving, Elie hasn't been missed yet.

I still say this renaissance truly started the night Olajuwon was suspended in Sacramento. That was the night a lot of people decisively took it upon themselves to bring something to the party. And the aggressive approach continued after Olajuwon came back.

What's that they say about confidence breeding confidence?

April 14

For the Rockets, it just keeps getting better and better.

The guards are getting their second wind and so is Horry. It has taken this long for Horry to recover from the emotional scars of The Trade That Wasn't. Plus, Horry must have learned a lesson from that scenario: If he won't take the outside shot, the Rockets will find somebody who will.

Tonight, Horry scored a career-high 30 points against Sacramento, including 22 in the fourth quarter. He was 10 of 14 from the floor and had a career-high 14 rebounds.

Sean who?

"Teams are going to learn to stop taking the gamble that we won't hit the open shot," Smith said. "They left Robert open, and he hit the lottery."

San Antonio can forget it now.

The Rockets' magic number for clinching the Midwest Division is down to two.

April 15

After going virtually an entire season without a traditional general manager, Les Alexander finally may have his man.

During last night's Rockets-Sacramento game, I heard the club may be zeroing in on Minnesota Assistant Coach Bob Weinhauer as the man to fill the vice president of basketball operations opening. I cornered Alexander in the hallway, and the owner confirmed the rumor's validity.

"He (Weinhauer) is a hard-working guy, and we've received a lot of positive reports on him," Les said. "We'll see."

On the flight to Seattle today, I asked Tomjanovich about Weinhauer. Tomjanovich provided a ringing endorsement.

Maybe, just maybe, this on-again, off-again, eight-month search is about to end.

An NBA front office can only operate on automatic pilot for so long.

April 16

Leave it to George Karl.

Even before today's Rockets-Sonics game commenced, Karl had created controversy.

Karl recently took some verbal jabs at Tomjanovich in an *Esquire Magazine* article. Those quotes were reprinted in a Seattle newspaper as the Rockets arrived in town.

"All I know is, last year he (Tomjanovich) had one play," Karl was quoted as saying. "Throw it to Hakeem. All the other plays he ran didn't work. All that pick-and-roll and all those other things he thinks are real cute? We took him out of everything they had."

Before tip-off, Karl tried to explain the context of those comments.

Early in the season, Karl said Tomjanovich had talked about how the Rockets play straight-up defense and don't rely on gimmicks like some other teams. Karl felt it was a slap against Seattle's chaotic defensive style and tried to express that sentiment in the *Esquire* article.

"What I said was a defense mechanism against what Rudy had said," Karl commented. "I wasn't intending to criticize Rudy . . . I was simply defending my team by pointing out that our particular defensive style stopped things Houston was doing offensively."

The Sonics stopped the Rockets again today, 100–97. That means the Sonics are a virtual lock for the No. 1 playoff seed in the West.

But the Rockets felt better when they retreated to their locker room and watched the final seconds of the Suns' win over San Antonio. Houston's magic number for clinching the division is down to one.

Looks like the road to the NBA Finals will go through Seattle. For many reasons, the Rockets are looking forward to that pit stop.

April 17

Best in the Midwest? You bet.

The Rockets did it with flair tonight in Portland, and the NBA should be "four"-warned that Houston is primed for the playoffs. Smith and Maxwell each had a four-point play as the Rockets repeated as Midwest champs with a 119–110 victory.

It was a long, hard road to travel. San Antonio made a strong move. Utah made a strong move. But over the course of 82 games, the cream always rises to the top.

And the cream of the Midwest crop was the team from Houston.

"When we gathered for training camp in Galveston, we said we were going to play hard, play smart and play together," Tomjanovich said. "This team has done that, and the result is a division title. I think we did it with class."

There were a lot of contented smiles in the Rockets locker room as players tried on shirts that read "1994 Midwest Division champions." But nobody was pouring champagne.

A division title is nice, but a Western Conference title and an NBA title represent the real carrots at the end of the string.

"This is like an appetizer," Olajuwon said. "The appetizer tastes good. But now we're looking forward to the main course."

On the long flight from Portland to San Antonio, Tomjanovich had a chance to reflect on what his team has just accomplished. It's the first time a Houston team in a major professional sport has produced back-to-back division titles.

"You appreciate them for different reasons," Tomjanvoich said. "This year, we were like the quarter-miler who has the lead. The field catches up and then it's a matter of gutting it out to win at the end. I couldn't be prouder of this team."

The Rockets have had a late 7–1 spurt while the Spurs were losing six of seven. Houston's division title means the MVP award for Olajuwon is a lock.

During today's plane ride, some members of the travel party were playing the "What If" game. What if the Horry for Elliott trade had gone through?

Would the Rockets have finished in first place?

"Stability equals success," Smith said.

Tomjanovich wants to make sure Houston stays ahead of all the Eastern Conference teams, so that Houston would have home-court advantage just in case it should reach the NBA Finals. Once the team locks up the home-court edge against every team except Seattle, it will be time to start resting the regulars for the playoffs.

For the first time in a long time, the Rockets can relax a bit.

Tonight is the start of the Fiesta celebration in San Antonio.

The Rockets should join the merriment. They've earned it.

April 19

Too little, too late for the San Antonio Spurs.

With 32,807 fans at the Alamodome waving placards that said "MVP 50", the Spurs defeated the Rockets tonight 90–80. The placards represented a final, desperate campaign drive for Robinson to win MVP. But even Lucas knows that's not going to happen. Lucas admitted afterward that San Antonio's recent 1–6 slide likely doomed Robinson's MVP chances.

"We lost focus for a minute, and it probably cost David the MVP award," Lucas said.

The 57–22 Rockets will have to win their final three games to hit the 60 plateau. But that numerical milestone pales in comparison to the more important goal of getting Olajuwon and his starting mates some rest.

"We have to draw the line between being competitive and the wear-and-tear factor," Tomjanovich said. "I don't want guys to play long minutes at the expense of being ready for the playoffs."

The trip is over. Time for the Rockets to go home and watch another Midwest Division banner rise to the rafters of The Summit.

April 20

The last big order of business this week is determining the play-off roster. Once postseason plays begins, the 12-man roster cannot be changed. With the deadline for submitting the playoff roster set for April 25 at 3 p.m., Tomjanovich and his staff have some significant decisions to make.

Bullard has had difficulty bouncing back from a strained calf muscle. Herrera is plagued by tendinitis in both knees and Elie—although his rehab is said to be on schedule—remains a question mark.

The Rockets are scrambling to give themselves as many options as possible. Yesterday, they placed Bullard on the injured list and signed an eager-beaver swingman, Chris Jent. He's a guy who almost joined the Rockets in February. When the 2-for-1 deal with Detroit was announced, Jent was called up from Columbus of the CBA to fill the open spot on the Houston roster. But Jent's excitement turned to disappointment when the deal was voided and Jent had to go back to the CBA.

I like this attention to detail. It shows the basketball staff is on the ball.

Most clubs wouldn't even bother tinkering with the bottom end of the roster this late in the year, figuring that only seven or eight guys are going to figure prominently in the playoffs anyway.

Tomjanovich is intent on putting together the best 12-man roster he can for the war ahead. A role player might be able to contribute a minute here or one big play there. And one key moment could be the difference between winning and losing a series.

Right now, Jent is a wide-eyed newcomer living for the moment. He has no idea whether he will be here a few days, a few weeks, a few months or a few years.

The fine-tuning of the roster continued today. Before the Rockets blasted Dallas 126–100, the club announced it has signed veteran center Earl Cureton, who recently has been with Magic Johnson's traveling All-Stars and with Sioux Falls in the CBA.

Cureton arrived at The Summit moments before tip-off. Two minutes had elapsed in the first period before he was suited up and on the bench.

The Rockets carried young frontliners Eric Riley and Richard Petruska for nearly an entire regular season, but the coaching staff believes a frontline veteran with strong character and championship experience is required for the playoffs.

Cureton played for the '82–'83 world champion Sixers. In times of playoff stress, he will be able to guide the younger, emotional players. The Rockets had a wise old veteran named Tree Rollins last year. He was a great influence in the locker room and could provide brief quality stretches on the court.

Ash, the scout who recommended Robinson earlier this month, believes Cureton will be a good pickup.

"Cureton is a guy with playoff experience," Tomjanovich said. "We just have to cover all of the bases. All of our reports indicate Earl is the type of guy we want (in the playoffs)."

If you can't have Rollins, maybe Cureton is the next best thing.

Lonnie Cooper, the Atlanta-based agent for Weinhauer, flew to Houston today for a meeting with Alexander.

If contract terms can be worked out, the Rockets will finally have a vice president of basketball operations.

"Everything I've heard about Bob has been extremely positive," Tomjanovich said as the Rockets prepared for their final regular-season road game in Dallas. "Nobody works harder. He has had experience with that kind of (front-office job), and he also understands the problems of a coach."

I've spoken with Weinhauer several times on the telephone in recent days. He can't officially comment on a possible position with the Rockets until his duties with the Timberwolves are completed this weekend. But there's no doubt that Bob considers the Houston opening an outstanding opportunity.

Weinhauer seems like a good guy. I hope this deal gets done.

April 24

Game No. 82 meant nothing, but a sellout crowd of 16,611 showed up to see the Midwest Division championship banner hoisted to The Summit's rafters.

As the burgundy-and-gold cloth was being raised between the first and second quarters of the Rockets-Denver game, this entire season flashed before my eyes.

Yeah, the playoffs are the big item in the NBA.

But it's a special accomplishment to win a division. It means you came through a test of endurance. The regular season is an endless blur of hotel rooms, bus rides, plane rides and practices. There are pratfalls at every turn and every team will have its "storms," as Tomjanovich puts it.

The 58–24 Rockets went through their shaky periods, with the complaints about playing time, the trade furor and the stern rushes of San Antonio and Utah.

This team could have easily splintered but didn't.

And the reward is that piece of cloth that went to the rafters today. Regardless of what happens in the playoffs, nobody can take away the significance of that '93–'94 division title banner.

It is a testament to the Rockets' resolve.

April 25

The Rockets' coaching staff met well into the night and again this morning regarding the playoff roster. The decision: Cureton, Jent and Elie will dress out; Riley, Robinson and Petruska won't.

In a show of team camaraderie, the three players left off the active roster have been advised they will continue to practice and travel with the team. Today's news was particularly delightful to Jent and Cureton. Before April 19, both were CBA players. Now, they're on the roster of a team that thinks it can win a championship.

After the roster was finalized, the Rockets headed for Galveston tonight to begin preparations for the first-round series against Portland.

Since Houston whipped Portland 4–0 in the regular season, most people seem to think the Rockets will dismiss Portland with relative ease in this best-of-five series.

I don't think it's going to be easy.

First of all, the Blazers didn't have center Chris Dudley for most of the regular season. Dudley is coming back for the playoffs, and that means natural forwards Buck Williams and Clifford Robinson won't have to play out of position.

Portland still has the same nucleus that went to the Finals in 1990 and 1992. Clyde Drexler, Williams, Terry Porter and Jerome Kersey may not be as quick and athletic as they were a couple of years ago, but this team still has heart, pride and talent.

I'm picking the Rockets to win it 3–2.

Say hello to playoff pressure.

April 26

The theme for our playoff Special Section in *The Houston Post* is "What It Takes To Win It All." I sat down with Rudy and asked for his insights into how playoff basketball is different from regular-season basketball.

"You definitely have to be able to adjust," he said. "That's the biggest part of playoff basketball. The opponent is going to know all your strengths, probably know all your calls. You've got to be able to go out there and say, 'This is what we've done all year—they aren't going to let us do that.' So you fine-tune this and adjust that.

"If you can do it, you're going to get through the series. If you can't be adaptable, it's going to be tough."

Tomjanovich had other points to make regarding the keys to play-off success. I wound up with a list of five basic ingredients that would put a team within reach of the Larry O'Brien Trophy:

1) Adjustments: With intensified scouting, few teams score on their first option.

2) Defensive Intensity: No letdowns on "D" for 48 minutes. It's the common denominator for thriving playoffs teams.

3) Poise Under Pressure: The opponent turns up the heat and so does the media. Who can handle it best?

4) Home-Court Advantages: Yes, the regular season means something. When the talent gap narrows, home court is often the difference.

5) Peak Performances: The coaches and scouts can only do so much. It inevitably boils down to who has the most players taking their games to a higher level.

Want to win it all? Better count on going 5-for-5.

April 27

The Rockets' coaches always love it when the other team provides them with bulletin-board material. Any juicy quote from the opposing camp that can be used for additional motivation is welcomed.

Well, the coaches should be happy today. Get out the yellow Hi-Liter.

Word has filtered in from the Portland camp that Robinson is going on the offensive. With Dudley available to play center, Coach Rick Adelman is thinking about using Robinson at small forward against Horry.

"If that happens, I'll kill Horry," Robinson said. "You can quote me on that. I don't care. I would kill him."

After today's workout in Galveston, Horry met that verbal barrage in an aggressive manner.

"I think I play against a lot of small forwards better than him, like Scottie Pippen and Dominique Wilkins," Horry retorted. "So, I'm not going to worry about what he says. I just have to go out and play.

"He's supposed to feel that way about me, and I'm supposed to feel that way about him. No player in the NBA should feel another can stop him. You're supposed to have the confidence and drive to get the job done."

Robinson is an outstanding player, but I like Horry's chances in this series. Last year at this time, Horry's knees ached so badly he could barely run up and down the floor.

Going into this year's playoffs, Horry is physically and mentally ready. The aborted trade to Detroit now seems like it happened in another lifetime. The only time Horry thinks about it is when some out-of-town reporter approaches him, looking for the easy angle.

Maybe Clifford Robinson isn't aware of all this.

The Rockets are fidgety today. They're tired of the pre-series hype and ready to put that nervous energy to good use.

The quest for glory begins tomorrow. Fifteen victories would mean a world championship, but the Houston players have tunnel vision. They just want one "break the ice" victory to get this Playoff Express rolling.

"Enough talking, enough practice," Elie said. "This team is ready. It's time for the show."

I'll agree the starters are ready, but I'm not sure the whole team is.

Going into Game 1, there are enough questions concerning the bench to start a quiz show.

Elie has practiced this week, but nobody can say for sure how he'll react after a month on the injured list. Herrera hasn't played lately, nor has Bullard. Cureton and Jent are new to the Rockets, and Cassell is about to find out that the intensity level of the playoffs is several notches above regular-season intensity.

I don't know about this bench.

Rudy T has used the same pregame routine all year. He writes his game notes on the blackboard in the Rockets' locker room, then ventures out to press row to do his radio show with Gene Peterson. When that is over, the coach shoots the breeze with the print media until exactly 39 minutes before tip-off.

As soon as the arena clock hits 39:00, Rudy will say "gotta go to work" and head back to the locker room.

The routine didn't change for Game 1 of the playoffs.

During the informal print media gathering tonight, Rudy said he felt the team had prepared well for the Blazers.

"But you still have to shoot the ball," Tomjanovich said. "If the ball doesn't go in, you don't look good."

In Game 1, the ball went in.

So much for the Blazers' notion that they could win this series simply by neutralizing Olajuwon.

The Blazers persistently double-teamed Olajuwon, and the Houston supporting cast came through in grand fashion. Houston shot .533 from the floor and hit 9 of 16 shots from three-point range. Maxwell was particularly effective, hitting for 24 points, including 5 of 8 three-pointers. When Drexler roamed away to help on Olajuwon, Maxwell kept delivering long-range daggers to Portland's heart.

"Vernon is just a crunch-time player," Tomjanovich said. "He has broken games open like that many times before."

The Rockets led by 19 points early in the second quarter, but Portland received masterful offensive performances from Drexler and Porter to pull ahead by three early in the fourth period.

"We never panicked," Elie said. "It was gut-check time, and our defense came through."

With Houston up two in the final five minutes, Maxwell hit two treys and two medium-range jumpers in a 3:23 span. Rockets 114, Blazers 104.

The pressure on the home team in Game 1 of a best-of-five series is enormous. Lose the game and a whole season's worth of good work is obliterated.

That big sigh of relief I thought I heard around 11 p.m. must have come from the vicinity of the Rockets' locker room.

Then again, maybe it came from the front office.

The Rockets finally made it official today. Weinhauer is the new vice president of basketball operations.

It only took eight months to fill the job.

April 30

Drexler didn't let the Game 1 loss get him down. On a rainy Saturday, he spent his morning relaxing at the Houston Open golf tournament.

By the time the Blazers' main man arrived at The Summit for an afternoon practice, he had a plan for how Portland could even the series in Game 2 and steal the home-court advantage.

"We have to change our strategy," Drexler said. "We drop way down to cover Hakeem and Maxwell shoots so quick. It's a matter of staying closer to home and not paying so much attention to Hakeem. That's a scary thought."

After Drexler made that statement, I began to wonder if Adelman would get radical in his defensive adjustment. Whenever Olajuwon received single coverage in the regular season, he generally racked up points as though he were playing a pinball machine.

Olajuwon scored 26 points in Game 1, but Adelman was impressed by Dudley's defensive work in 18 minutes.

Maybe Adelman thinks the answer is to give Olajuwon 30 or 35 points with single coverage, which might allow Portland's defense to hold everybody else in check.

Are the Blazers really going to do an about-face by challenging Olajuwon as a scorer?

As Drexler admitted, that's a scary thought.

May 1

Some things you just shouldn't do, as the late Jim Croce once suggested. You don't tug on Superman's cape. You don't spit into the wind. You don't pull the mask off the Lone Ranger . . . and you don't play Olajuwon with one man if that man isn't named Pat Ewing, David Robinson or Shaquille O'Neal.

Sure enough, the Blazers went with single coverage on Olajuwon in Game 2, and it was akin to pouring gasoline on an open fire. One-on-one was loads of fun for Olajuwon, who exploded for 46 points in Houston's 115–104 victory.

"When teams play me one-on-one, it's an opportunity," Olajuwon said.

Olajuwon is so used to being double-teamed he had to adjust his game and focus on taking the easy shot. He was only 9 of 21 at the half but then hit 7 of his last 9 shots and finished 13 of 18 from the foul line.

Asked about the Blazers' dubious strategy, Olajuwon turned into a diplomat.

"It was a nice try," he said.

The Rockets are going to Portland with a 2–0 lead, and it's turning into a pick-your-poison series for the Blazers. If they crowd Olajuwon, the perimeter troops hit the threes. If they play it straight, Olajuwon goes wild.

As good as he was offensively tonight, Olajuwon's most stunning play came on defense.

The Rockets were up 104–98 when Olajuwon's pass was picked off by Rod Strickland for what seemed like a cinch breakaway.

But when Olajuwon makes a mistake, he tends to erase it. Starting from midcourt, Olajuwon did his Carl Lewis sprinter/long jump imitation. He chased down Strickland and lunged from behind for a clean block as Strickland was about to cut Houston's lead to four.

"He looked like a gazelle," Adelman marveled. "I don't know how he got there."

And I don't know what the Blazers are going to do now.

Nobody could have convinced me the Rockets would average 114.5 points through two playoff games. Unless Portland comes up with some answers, it's going to be a short trip to the lush Pacific Northwest.

May 2

It must have been a particularly tough trip home for Adelman.

Some members of the Portland media are speculating he could be down to his last game as the Blazers' coach because of a power struggle within the Portland organization.

Sad.

Adelman is a class guy and a good coach. This is a commentary on how fickle the NBA industry can be. Adelman has won two of the last four Western Conference championships, yet his job may be on the line if his team doesn't get past the Rockets.

Adelman didn't have his *real* team all season. Without the services of the desired starting center, Portland still won 47 games.

I wonder how the Blazers will respond tomorrow in Game 3. Will they play with pride and fight for their embattled coach? Or will they roll over?

I've got to think the former will be true. This corps of Portland veterans has been through too much to give up without a serious fight.

The Rockets' motivation for sweeping the series involves the rest factor. Houston is hopeful of a 3–0 quickie over Portland, coupled with a long Golden State/Phoenix series. This combination would give Houston a significant rest advantage for the second round.

If the Rockets don't win Game 3 Tuesday, they'll have to hang out on the road until Game 4 Friday night.

It's pretty here in Portland. From their downtown hotel, the Rockets get a picturesque view of the Willamette River and their walking-distance choice of restaurants featuring fresh, succulent salmon.

But with all due respect to the Portland Chamber of Commerce, I'm sure the the Rockets don't want to fully unpack their bags.

The Rockets showed up for Game 3 without their team personality.

Defense has been Houston's foundation for victory all year, but there were some serious cracks in the slab as the Blazers stayed alive with a 118–115 victory. Strickland penetrated at will, Williams hit 9 of 10 shots and Portland rang up an alarming 96 points in the opening three quarters.

"Our defense was weak," Olajuwon said. "There is no way you can win on the road giving them that much opportunity to score. We gave up too much penetration."

As bad as they were defensively, the Rockets still made a bid to pull the game out with some typical Maxwell heroics. The Blazers were up 116–112 when Vernon hit a three-pointer with 12.6 seconds remaining. Porter missed one of two free throws with 8.3 seconds to go, but Maxwell made a *faux pas* by firing an off-balance three-point attempt when he had Olajuwon open in the low post for a possible tying shot.

Maxwell admitted after the game he thought the Rockets were down by three points instead of two when he fired the airball trey.

"I lost track of the score," Maxwell said. "If I had known we were down two, I would have given the ball to Hakeem because he had his man on his back. I wish I could have it back. But I played my butt off."

I give Vernon credit for facing the media and owning up to his mistake. In the heat of the battle—when Porter missed one of the two free throws with 8.3 remaining—it simply didn't register in Maxwell's mind.

A lot of players wouldn't have offered the real story.

Vernon showed me a lot. But the Rockets' defense didn't.

Amazingly, Houston didn't score a point off turnovers or blocked shots in Game 3. That's the definitive signal the Houston defense didn't have its usual bite.

"The positive sign is that as bad as we played defensively, we still had a chance to win," Tomjanovich said. "We just have to get back in character. Team defense is what got us here, and team defense is what has to carry us through this series."

Guess I'd better unpack now. We're going to be in Portland awhile.

Jim Preston

The Houston Rocket starters stand united in their successful quest for a championship.

Robert Seale

The
Houston
Rockets

1994 NBA Champions

Hakeem Olajuwon, left, had a triple crown season, winning an NBA title, and being selected League Most Valuable Player and Defensive Player of the Year.

The Season
A Rollercoaster Ride to the Playoffs

Otis Thorpe, right, and his team-mates send their season-opening opponent, the New Jersey Nets, sprawling at The Summit on Nov. 5 as The Streak begins.

Adrees Latif

Rex Curry

The three-time defending champion Chicago Bulls got an early lesson that the Rockets were the new powers on the NBA block when they met in November.

The infamous midseason trade that wasn't would have had the Rockets' Robert Horry and Detroit's Sean Elliott trading uniforms.

Adrees Latif

Rex Curry

Above, Coach Rudy Tomjanovich was seldom up in arms over his team's play this season.

John Makely

The Rockets' perfect 15-0 start went up in flames in Atlanta.

The Best
A Championship Cast

John Makely

Otis Thorpe slams another one through.

Adrees Latif

Kenny Smith is at his best on the offensive prowl.

Robert Seale

Forward Robert Horry came through at both ends of the court.

Adrees Latif

Supercharged Vernon Maxwell kept the team on the ball during lulls.

Adrees Latif

Hakeem Olajuwon silenced any arguments with David Robinson over who was the NBA's best.

Adrees Latif

Off-season acquisition Mario Elie came through off the bench.

Robert Seale

Carl Herrera provided
invaluable front line relief.

Ira Strickstein

The Rockets circle the defensive wagons around the Blazers' Harvey Grant at The Summit.

Portland:
The First Step

Rockets 3
Trailblazers 1

Vernon Maxwell was
more than willing to
hit the hardwood in
pursuit of a victory.

Robert Seale

Phoenix:
Big Hurdle Falls

Rockets 4
Suns 3

Hakeem Olajuwon
gets a hand on the ball
as Cedric Ceballos
goes up for a shot,
sandwiching the Sun's
Oliver Miller.

Robert Seale

John Makely

Suns superstar Charles Barkley didn't much care for the Rockets' trademark blanket defense.

Utah:
Best in the West

Rockets 4
Jazz 1

Sam Cassell and
Otis Thorpe, right,
make a defensive
sandwich of Jazz
star Karl Malone.

Ira Strickstein

Adrees Latif

An emotional Mario Elie
celebrated another win as his
team leaped into the NBA
Finals.

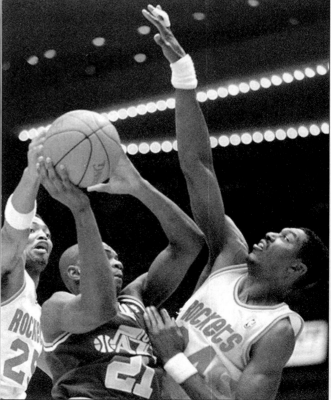

Robert Horry
and Hakeem
Olajuwon reject
a shot by Utah's
David Benoit.

Adrees Latif

Game 1
Rockets 85   Knicks 78

John Makely

Charles Smith gets a wake-up call from Robert Horry.

John Makely

Thorpe's victory yell after a slam.

Robert Seale

Hakeem Olajuwon and Patrick Ewing jump for the opening tip-off in Game 1 at The Summit.

The NBA Finals

NBA Finals
Game 2
Knicks 91   Rockets 83

John Makely

Physical contact was the norm in the Finals.

John Makely

Otis Thorpe soars over John Starks to the net.

John Makely

Knicks' Charles Smith pulls in a loose ball as New York rebounds for a win to tie the series.

Above, high-flying Robert Horry soars for a basket that boosts the Rockets and grounds the Knicks at The Garden.

NBA Finals
Game 3
Rockets 93   Knicks 89

Guard Sam Cassell takes the ball right at Patrick Ewing, driving the Rockets to a 2-1 series lead.

Robert Seale

The headlock by Charles Smith was mild compared to the bruising awaiting Robert Horry.

NBA Finals
Game 4

Knicks 91   Rockets 82

The Rockets' bench as the game
came to a disappointing end told
the story of how they let this one
get away to tie the series at 2.

John Makely

John Makely

NBA Finals
Game 5

Knicks 91   Rockets 84

Hakeem Olajuwon wrestles for the ball, giving an elbow shot to Anthony Mason. Another big night from the Dream was not enough for a win.

John Makely

Unhappy with a call, an emotionally charged Rudy Tomjanovich was unable to rally his team for a road win.

Scrambling for a loose ball, New York's Charles Oakley leaves Otis Thorpe sprawled on The Garden floor.

John Makely

NBA Finals
Game 6
Rockets 86   Knicks 84

Ira Strickstein

A clutch 3-pointer brings cheers for Smith.

Ira Strickstein

Even smothered by the Rockets Starks scored 27.

Ira Strickstein

A desperation 3-pointer by John Starks is tipped by Hakeem Olajuwon as the clocks runs out.

Ira Strickstein

Robert Horry stuffed a left-handed slam dunk in the face of Knicks center Patrick Ewing.

John Makely

As time ran out on New York, Sam Cassell celebrated winning an NBA title in his rookie season in Houston.

Ira Strickstein

On the floor, Maxwell celebrated a closing 3-pointer.

NBA Finals
Game 7
Rockets 90   Knicks 84

John Makely

Surrounded by the Houston Rockets, NBA Commissioner David Stern prepares to present the championship trophy in The Summit, kicking off a celebration all over the city.

The Larry O'Brien NBA Championship Trophy glistens with the evening Houston skyline.

Craig Hartley

CHAMP CITY!

May 4

When things go wrong, it seems as though Kenny Smith is usually the eye of the storm.

I called home today and learned the Strickland versus Smith matchup had become the hot issue on the KTRH call-in show. Fans were upset that Strickland owned the lane in Game 3 while delivering 25 points and 15 assists. Through three games, Strickland is averaging 22.7 points and 10.7 assists.

Stop Strickland. That has become the war cry.

"As a team, we didn't come with the same kind of defensive effort that we showed in the first two games," Smith said. "And some of us have to take it personally, especially myself."

There's no way Smith or even Cassell—a better backcourt defender—can totally deny Strickland's penetration. Strickland is one of the top drive-and-dish guards in the league.

"It's not strictly a one-on-one deal," Tomjanovich said. "There were major breakdowns in our whole defensive system. Our defense is based on help, and we weren't helping as a five-man unit. Defensively, the game film was a horrible sight."

Although they still lead this series 2–1, the Rockets have dug themselves a hole by stinking it up defensively in Game 3. Tonight, Phoenix completed a 3–0 series sweep over Golden State as Barkley went wild with 56 points.

Don Nelson tried to do to Barkley what Adelman tried to do against Olajuwon in Game 2. The Warriors thought they could win by single-covering Barkley and stopping everybody else. It didn't work.

Against a superstar, you've got to mix up the defenses so the main man doesn't get into a rhythm. It's like a pitcher needing to change speeds to keep the big hitter confused and off-stride.

Barkley knew the Warriors weren't coming with help, so he could make his moves in a comfort zone. He just kept scoring and scoring and scoring.

Thus, Phoenix is in a great position from the standpoint of rest.

Regardless of which team they play in the second round, the Suns are going to start that series as the fresher club.

The Rockets definitely have a problem in terms of the overall playoff picture. If they win Game 4 Friday night, they will have to make a long red-eye journey home and start the next series Sunday afternoon as a fatigued team. If the series with the Blazers goes to Game 5 . . . well, anything could happen in a one-game scenario. Houston found that out last year when it took a dramatic three-pointer by Maxwell in the final minute of Game 5 to lift Houston past the Clippers.

Bottom line, the Phoenix Suns have to feel pretty good right now.

May 5

Vernon Alert, Vernon Alert.

It happened well after the media availability session today. I was working on my Game 4 advance story when Channel 2 producer Rick McFarland called me in my hotel room.

"We just talked to Vernon," McFarland said. "He's going to the hospital for X-rays on his shooting hand."

Nobody with the Rockets had said anything about a Maxwell injury. But Maxwell had told Channel 2 anchorman Craig Roberts he'd have to postpone a scheduled hotel lobby interview until he returned from the hospital. He had suffered a bruised third knuckle on his shooting hand in Game 3 and aggravated it in Wednesday's practice.

"It hurts like crazy," Maxwell said after returning from the hospital. X-rays had proven negative, but the pain was intense.

"If the game had been today," he added, "I wouldn't have been able to play. I couldn't shoot or dribble."

Just what the Rockets didn't need. If Maxwell's shooting touch is off tomorrow, it could be the edge Portland needs to take this series to the limit.

Adelman was confident today. He just wants to get this series back to Houston. All the pressure would be on the heavily favored Rockets if that were to happen.

"In a one-game deal, that ball has a tendency to feel a little heavier," Adelman said. "You never know what might happen . . . foul trouble, injuries, a cold shooting streak. Every game we've played at The Summit this year, we've had a chance to win."

The Rockets are getting antsy with the two-day break between games. Staying in Portland from Monday through Friday night represents culture shock for a group used to hopping from city to city. There's only so many times you can visit Portland's Nike Employee Store, where players are offered huge discounts on athletic wearing apparel.

"My fingers ache from flicking the remote control on the television in my room," Brooks quipped. "I've been 'Around The World' with CNN about 15 times."

I'm sensing the team is mad at itself for creating this extended odyssey by not taking care of business in Game 3. The players have seen the video mistakes over and over, and their legs will be fresh for tomorrow's game.

The Rockets will come with full force. They're ready to win the game, climb on a plane and wave goodbye to Oregon.

May 6

Maxwell's OK and so are the Rockets.

Houston put forth tremendous defensive energy early in Game 4 and held on late for a 92–89 triumph and a 3–1 series victory. I've seen this team have some great defensive stretches this year, but the first quarter tonight was as good as it gets.

The Rockets looked like a red tornado flying through Memorial Coliseum. The stunned Blazers hit only 4 of 26 shots in the quarter and trailed 27–13 after one period. Although it got hairy for Houston in the second half, the sheer will to win pulled the Rockets through.

The crowd noise was deafening after Strickland hit two free throws to pull Portland within 89–87 with 36 seconds remaining. But then the Rockets got the big play and the big call to put them over the top. Olajuwon missed a shot but followed and knocked the ball off a Blazer and out-of-bounds with 11 seconds remaining.

The Rockets hung on with free throws, and Strickland's potential-tying trey missed at the buzzer. Adelman and Tomjanovich embraced at midcourt, and the Rockets romped off the floor with Phase I of their grand plan having been accomplished.

"I'm drained," Tomajanovich said. "We talked about getting back our defensive identity. It's the only way we can win. The early defense set the tone for the whole game. It turned into a dogfight, but our guys hung in and did what it took to win."

Clifford Robinson was miserable in Game 4, finishing just 3 of 15 from the floor. Rememember that pre-series quote when Robinson said he would "kill" Horry? Well, the statistics show Horry with a .590 field-goal percentage in this series, compared to Robinson's .412.

"I've been reincarnated," Horry said with a smile.

Maxwell hit only 3 of 10 shots with his bruised shooting hand, but the other aspects of his game were sound. The doctors are saying the soreness in Maxwell's hand should go away during the next series.

The Rockets had only about an hour to celebrate their first-round victory. Houston has to fly home tonight because the start of the Phoenix series is only 38 hours away.

I was among the last to leave Memorial Coliseum.

It was eerily quiet, in contrast to the pandemonium that had reigned a couple of hours earlier. This was the end of an era in Portland. Adelman probably would be fired. And the pained looks on the faces of aging warriors such as Drexler, Porter, Williams and Kersey were a commentary about what might have been.

This proud Portland team had been so close to a championship dream in 1990, 1991 and 1992. Now, the players knew the run was over.

The thought strikes me that in a couple of years, the Rockets will be where the Blazers are now. Olajuwon, Thorpe, Maxwell and Smith won't have young legs forever.

Houston should learn something from Portland's sad saga.

The Rockets had better realize the importance of seizing the championship moment. Hey, guys . . . the window of opportunity doesn't stay open indefinitely.

May 7

Because I'd been so consumed with the Rockets-Blazers series, I hadn't paid much attention to what was going on with Denver and Seattle.

I knew the Nuggets won twice at McNichols Sports Arena to force a Game 5, but I figured—like 99.99 percent of the prognosticators—that Seattle would win easily in a decisive game at home.

It just seemed inevitable that after a 63–19 regular season, the Sonics would represent the definitive road block for either Phoenix or Houston in the Western Conference.

But as I was driving in from Intercontinental Airport late this afternoon, I turned on the radio just as KTRH's Charlie Palillo was delivering the shocking news: Denver led Seattle by two with the Sonics down to a make-or-break possession.

I was on Highway 59 near downtown, and it's a good thing I didn't run through any speed traps. My foot pushed harder on the accelerator because I wanted to get to The Summit and check the Rockets' immediate reaction to a Sonics' fall from grace.

Oops, false alarm. The news came that the Sonics had scored on a rebound basket with less than one second left. No way they will lose it now, I figured. So I slowed down and forgot all about it.

By the time I parked and walked into The Summit, media members were converging in the hallway.

"Denver won in overtime," somebody said.

I looked at the television set, and Dikembe Mutombo was reclining under the basket, with the ball in his hands and a big smile on his face.

Seattle was out! Wonder what that cocky George Karl is saying now?

Until that moment, the idea of a Houston championship had seemed, to me, like a hazy, distant goal. I had figured the Rockets would be hard-pressed to get past Seattle without home-court advantage.

But now, the Rockets were in a position to do more than just dream the impossible dream.

The Rockets' players had just begun to arrive at The Summit. The Suns had watched the end of the game in their locker room, and the outcome left Barkley joyous.

"This series is huge now," Barkley said.

That it is.

The bottom line is that if Houston wins all its home games, the Rockets will be world champions.

"That sounds good, but you've still got to get it done," Tomjanovich said. "Seattle was in that position, too."

Are the fates at work here?

Jordan retires. Seattles loses.

Some important issues are breaking the Rockets' way. Maybe this is the time for suffering Houston sports fans to exorcise the near-miss demons that have long haunted this city.

But it's not all sunshine and lollipops going into the Western Conference semifinals. Cassell threw a punch at Kersey in the Portland finale and has been suspended for tomorrow's game. The Rockets are still battling jet lag after flying all night to get back from the Pacific Northwest. Furthermore, there's going to be a different kind of pressure for the Rockets, now being recast as "the team to beat."

Oh, and one other thing. Phoenix is the hottest ballclub in the NBA.

May 8

Well, I guess it could be worse. The Rockets could be the Seattle SuperSonics and on vacation right now.

Those are the only words of consolation I can offer after the double-barreled dilemma down at The Summit today. The Rockets lost Game 1 to the Suns 91–87, blowing an 18-point first-half lead. The Rockets also touched off what's certain to be a major "Fan Flap" controversy.

If they forgot to call their mothers on Mother's Day, it was a complete washout.

The problems started early when the players came out for the opening tip-off and noticed about 3,000 empty seats. There were several theories floating about as to why that happened. Houston management has been doling out tickets series by series because the prices escalate from one round to the next. Because of the quick turnaround from the Portland series to the Phoenix series, there was some ticket-buying confusion.

The 2 p.m. starting time on Mother's Day also probably contributed to lackluster attendance. But the biggest factor of all, perhaps, was the notion that Rockets' Fever just hasn't warmed to a desirable temperature.

Houston attendance has been poor all year, considering the team's achievements. Today marks the third consecutive non-sellout of the playoffs.

"When people get excited, the game sells out," said John Thomas, the new vice president of business operations.

First, the game story. Then the fan story.

The Rockets had 50 shots inside nine feet and missed 23 of them. After building the 39–21 lead, Houston didn't get much done. The Suns were clearly playing with a higher energy level in the second half and that was the reward for finishing off their first-round opponent early.

The real fireworks came *after* the buzzer.

On a day when Rush Limbaugh came to see his good buddy Paul Westphal, the Rockets were wishing they had more friends.

"I don't think this city really wants to win a championship," Olajuwon said. "There was no excuse for that crowd. That's not why we lost, but support is a big part of it. The fans get everybody going, but tonight they had no fire. I couldn't believe it."

Maxwell, the most outspoken Rocket, chided himself for hitting just 1 of 9 shots. Then he chided the fans.

"Our fans are the worst," Maxwell said. "To hell with 'em. Can't even sell out a second-round playoff game. They are the worst, and you can write that."

This attendance issue is like the charter airline issue early in the year. Players have been suppressing their thoughts because they didn't want to react prematurely. But when somebody hits the pressure release button, the frustration comes bursting forth.

Tomorrow, the fans will have their say. You can count on that.

May 9

Yeah, this Fan Flap story has struck a raw nerve in the community.

Consequently, the Suns-Rockets series will have to stay on the backburner for awhile until the fans are through venting their feelings and flapping their wings.

The Houston Post began receiving calls on the matter early this morning, and a Channel 2 crew tore out for The Summit so it could get Olajuwon's second-day comments on the noon news. The station caught up with Olajuwon before practice. Never mind that the Rockets weren't supposed to be interviewed until after practice.

Several media members waited outside The Summit to interview fans who were coming up to the ticket office for Game 2 purchases.

I approached a man named David Lopez, who gave his perspective of the controversy.

Lopez thought the Rockets were speaking out of frustration after losing Game 1 at home. But Lopez thought the players had a point.

"People are kind of sitting around waiting for the Rockets or some other team to prove they are a championship team," Lopez said. "I don't think it works that way. I think you have to get *behind* the team and boost it to a championship."

Olajuwon, Maxwell and Elie had each criticized the Game 1 turnout, and nobody was backing down today. If their real motive is to stoke the pride of the Houston sports community, I would say they have succeeded beyond their wildest expectations.

An emotional environment has been created through all of this. And emotion is a crucial element for any team on a championship mission.

When Fan Flap began, I thought it was a bad omen for the Rockets. Conventional wisdom says you never want to create peripheral enemies and lose focus in the playoffs.

But if that's what it takes to get Houston fans riled up and in a passionate frame of mind, it may yet prove to be a big-picture blessing.

May 10

The fans have done their part. Game 2 sold out in a 45-minute frenzy.

But will the Rockets do their part by evening the series?

As the Fan Flap controversy begins to lose some of its steam, one fact is becoming self-evident: The Rockets had better win tomorrow or the fans will get indignant again and boo the players all the way to Phoenix.

We're either in for a lovefest or a hatefest tomorrow. This could be a highly volatile situation if the Rockets don't jump out early and back up their words with deeds.

Here's the feedback I'm getting in the community: "The Rockets want support? OK, but don't mess up. We'll give you our heart, but you'd damn well better not break it."

Rudy feels good about Game 2. He thought the defense was solid in Game 1. If Houston shoots better on fresh legs, the Rockets and their fans should be happy again.

"We lost the first game, but we know we can beat this team," Olajuwon said. "I'm so happy the fans regrouped right away (with the quick sellout). We'll try not to disappoint them."

Cassell will return to the rotation tomorrow, and Maxwell figures to shoot a lot better than the 1-for-9 line he posted in the series opener.

After riling the fans with his "to hell with 'em" comment, it would be just like Vernon to become a hero tomorrow. He thrives on controversy and claims he's ready for a big game.

"I live for this (bleep)," Maxwell said with a wink.

May 11

I looked up at the scoreboard with 6 minutes, 49 seconds remaining and figured it was safe to start writing my game-story lead. The score was Rockets 105, Suns 88.

I batted out a couple of sentences about the Rockets and their fans coming together in perfect harmony. I wrote that the series was tied 1–1, and the Rockets could regain the home-court advantage by getting a weekend split in Phoenix.

I looked up again and the Rockets were leading by 10 with 2:37 remaining. Still a lock, right? Wrong.

The Rockets were going against Sir Charles and going through the surreal. Houston did everything wrong, Phoenix capitalized and the next thing I knew, the game was headed to overtime.

My only salvation was the eraser button on my computer screen. All I could think of was the great turnaround line once used by Tommy Bonk, my *Houston Post* predecessor on the Rockets' beat:

"Given up for dead only paragraphs earlier . . ."

Well, given up for dead only paragraphs earlier, the Suns erased a 20-point deficit with 10 minutes remaining and defeated Houston 124–117 in overtime. It was the biggest fourth-quarter comeback in NBA playoff history and left shocked Houston sports fans with horrible visions of the Oilers' playoff loss in Buffalo on Jan. 3, 1993. In that one, Houston coughed up a 35–3 lead in the second half.

The Rockets scored 40 points in the third quarter and eight in the fourth quarter. Go figure.

When I walked over to do a pay-per-view television segment with Worrell, he looked like he had seen a ghost. Actually, he had seen five ghosts, and they were wearing the purple-and-orange colors of the Suns.

The Rockets couldn't have been any lower if they were ground-hogs. Seven months of heroics had seemingly gone up in smoke because of 10 hellish minutes.

In a stunned Rockets locker room, Bullard openly questioned the coaching staff by saying Houston got too predictable in the fourth quarter by constantly going to Olajuwon.

"We ran one play in the last 15 minutes," Bullard said. "We've got about 100 plays. If I had been in charge, I would have run a different play. That one wasn't working."

Meanwhile, Barkley was doing a TNT interview at courtside with Doug Collins. If any of the Rockets had seen and heard Barkley, they would have wanted to wipe that smug grin off his face.

Barkley told Collins none of the Rockets other than Olajuwon wanted to shoot the ball in the fourth quarter "so we got all over him like that cheap suit you're wearing."

The Rockets went right from the arena to Hobby Airport. Getting out of town through the veil of darkness was indeed the best policy for this situation.

Houston had simply begun to play the clock instead of the opponent. When you stop attacking in the NBA—especially against the highest-powered offensive team in the league—crazy things can happen.

Crazy things *did* happen.

Long after the last post-mortem had been written, Sophie Tomjanovich came strolling down the hallway from the Board Room. She was smiling and looked remarkably composed. And as she left through the back exit, I heard her tell the security guard in a pleasant voice: "See you Tuesday night (for Game 5)."

Game 5? I wondered if Sophie was being overly optimistic. All of a sudden, this series has "sweep" written all over it.

May 12

I didn't get much sleep last night. I kept tossing and turning, replaying in my mind those final few harrowing minutes of Game 2.

When I got up and started to pack for the trip to Phoenix, my wife Jackie asked a pertinent question, with a resigned look on her face.

"Why even bother?" she said.

I'm sure that's the prevailing sentiment in this heartbroken town. As I stuffed a weekend's worth of clothes in my bag, newspapers were hitting front lawns with a sickening thud.

"Choke City!" read the headlines.

Yes, Houston has been "buffaloed" once again. Let's see . . . is it tougher for a football team to blow a 35–3 third-quarter lead or a basketball team to blow a 20-point lead with 10 minutes remaining?

"There's only one difference between this and the Oilers-Buffalo game," I remarked to Jackie, a diehard Oilers fan. "The Oilers had no second chance. It was sudden death, and they had to carry that game with them through an entire off-season. At least the Rockets have another game to play. At least they can take solace that Game 2 won't be the last thing remembered about this season."

As I drove to the airport, I turned on the radio for some early feed-back. KSEV's John O'Reilly happened to be getting an analysis of the collapse from former Rockets guard Mike Newlin. The gist of the conversation dealt with the Rockets lack of a pure shooter.

When the Suns swarmed Olajuwon in the fourth quarter, Newlin felt other Houston players were reluctant to step up and take the big shot because nobody on the roster has a pure shooter's mentality.

But Newlin went on to say he wouldn't be surprised if the Rockets came back and won two games in Phoenix. He lauded the team's athleticism and defiant personality and felt that, contrary to popular opinion, the Rockets were not out of this series.

Newlin was eloquent in his analysis, and that word "defiant" stayed with me on the flight to Phoenix. Clearly, the Suns aren't world beaters, particularly at the defensive end of the floor. Great defensive teams don't fall behind by 18 and 20 points.

But will the Rockets be defiant enough to play through the tremendous psychological burden created by the Game 2 nightmare?

As soon as the media greeted the Rockets at America West Arena late this afternoon, it was obvious Tomjanovich had moved quickly to get the players back in the proper frame of mind. The first order of business was to eliminate the second-guessing that had gone on regarding play-calling down the stretch.

Tomjanovich had shown the team the evidence on videotape.

"Certain things were said in the heat of the moment that weren't true, and I understand that's going to happen sometimes," Tomjanovich said. "But I don't want our players wasting energy and creating doubt and confusion.

"We talked about it, so that we're all on the same page. The fact is, we diversified more in the fourth quarter than in the third. We ran seven pick-and-rolls in the fourth quarter. We had 13 open shots and made two."

Tomjanovich said the bulk of the offensive plays go through Olajuwon because he draws double coverage and creates open shots for teammates. However, the Rockets seemed to freeze in the fourth quarter because they were worried about taking shots too quickly with a seemingly insurmountable lead.

"The problem wasn't our play selection, it was the indecisiveness," Tomjanovich said. "As well as our guys shot in the Portland series, there's no reason for our guys to hesitate on the perimeter.

"What happened in Game 2 . . . I wouldn't wish it on anybody. But I'm not going to be a hypocrite and change an offense that won 58 games, beat Portland and got 18- and 20-point leads on a great team like the Suns. If you change your system, then you don't really believe in it. I believe in this team, and I believe we can bounce back in this series."

The question is, do the Rockets players believe it?

Everybody is talking brave and saying the right things today. But do they feel it in their hearts?

May 13

The Suns were standing in the runway, waiting to take the floor when Barkley poked his head into the huddle to deliver a motivational message.

"If you guys are goin' back to Texas, you're goin' without me," Barkley said.

Better call your travel agent, Charles. Your best-laid plans have gone astray.

The so-called "chokers" went wild tonight. In one of the most improbable scenarios in club history, the Rockets climbed on Maxwell's back and clawed back into this series. Maxwell exploded for 31 of his 34 points in the second half, and Houston came away with a 118–102 victory.

"People were holding up chickens and calling us chokers," Maxwell said. "We weren't going to stop until we proved everybody wrong. We showed everybody tonight we're one of the better clubs in the league."

Ah, sweet redemption. It was one hell of a Friday the 13th for the rejuvenated Rockets.

"This team has character," Tomjanovich said. "You don't win 58 games without having character. Fortunately, we got another chance. If the Oilers would have had another game right after Buffalo, they would have responded, too."

The Rockets had heard about the "Choke City" headlines in the Houston newspapers from family members and friends. After the ridicule, they bonded as a team like never before.

"Only 15 people—period—and their families believed we had a chance," Smith said.

This morning, the *Arizona Republic* ran a story about a sports psychologist named Frank Lodato of Newtown, Conn., who watched the Rockets blow leads in Games 1 and 2.

"When you are under pressure," Lodato said, "people will perform 30 percent better or 30 percent worse. That 60 percent is the difference between winning and losing."

The Rockets performed 30 percent better in the most pressurized situation of the season. A loss would have meant curtains, and Phoenix came in with only five home-court defeats all season.

Perhaps the most amazing aspect was that Houston fell behind 29–15 early in the second quarter. But the Rockets defense hung tough. Houston chipped within eight at the half, and then Maxwell exploded with a siege of drives and three-point bombs.

The Suns' only real offensive threat was Kevin Johnson, who had 38 points and 12 assists.

Barkley? He couldn't come through. With Thorpe providing the defensive muscle and forcing Barkley to shoot over the top, Super Mouth hit only 9 of 22 shots.

"I stunk," Barkley said. "Houston played good, but I don't want to give them too much credit. I take the blame for this."

The game ended with what many observers considered an outrageous display of poor sportsmanship by Danny Ainge. In the waning seconds, with Phoenix down 16, Ainge reared back and threw an inbounds pass that hit Elie in the face from point-blank range.

"The game was over, and I get a ball in the face," Elie seethed. "At close range, he could have broken my nose or knocked out some teeth. For what? It was totally uncalled for. I've never seen anybody get a 16-point play."

Elie said the Ainge episode would provide additional motivation for Game 4, and several other angry Rockets concurred.

Three games, three road victories. The Suns have to be thinking back to that 14-point lead and wondering how it got away.

Who's choking now?

May 14

The Houston Post publishes "Letters To The Sports Editor" every Sunday. Tomorrow's letters are going to be particularly enlightening. I think they pretty well reflect the mood of the fans after the Rockets' Game 2 collapse. Keep in mind these letters were written and mailed to the newspaper before Game 3:

1) "Houston is getting quite a name for itself around the nation. I was listening to a conversation between two guys on a bus in Chicago and one of them said: 'Houston was leading big, but blew it.' The other guy said: 'Who are you talking about—the Oilers, or the Astros, or the Rockets?' "

2) "The Houston Rockets are a joke and "Venom" Maxwell is a real jerk. Game 2 sold out and yet they blew it again. Who do you blame this time?"

3) "Do you think the Rockets are still wondering why they can't sell out The Summit? After the lack of intensity, concentration or anything else in the fourth quarter of that game Wednesday night, they'll be lucky to get Les Alexander to attend the rest of their games, which looks like it will only be two."

4) "Dear Rudy T: May I suggest that you rent Wizard of Oz. Sit all your players down and make them watch it. After the viewing, explain to them that—like the Tinman, Scarecrow and cowardly Lion—the heart, the brains and the courage comes from within and not from some wizard."

I wonder if these people will write again next week should the Rockets somehow win Game 4 and even this series.

May 15

Attention, fans. That Rockets bandwagon is now ready for reboarding, but climb on at your own risk.

Houston did the unthinkable today by completing a weekend sweep of the Suns in America West Arena. As the red-shirted visitors pranced into their locker room to celebrate a convincing 107–96 victory, Les Alexander was beaming like a proud papa.

"It's not Choke City, it's *Clutch City*," Alexander shouted.

Clutch City? Hey, not bad. If the Rockets keep playing like they played today, that label might stick.

The Rockets were spectacular in all phases, and Tomjanovich got very emotional while describing his team's resiliency.

"The city of Houston should be proud of this ballclub," Tomjanovich said. "These guys had their hearts ripped out in Game 2 and look how they responded. The Rockets aren't chokers . . . they are men."

Olajuwon had 28 points, 12 rebounds, eight assists and five blocks. His indomitable will to win was best illustrated as the Suns were mounting a last-gasp comeback. Johnson penetrated from the right side and dished to Barkley in the middle. Barkley took one big step and went up for what was supposed to be a monster slam that would have left Phoenix down four and turned the arena into a madhouse.

But Olajuwon met Barkley high above the rim. Last year's MVP against this year's likely MVP. Olajuwon fed Barkley a made-to-order Spaulding sandwich with an incredibly powerful, clean rejection.

Just as Olajuwon had turned Barkley's jam around, the Rockets had turned this series around.

Smith came up huge in Game 4 with 8-of-10 shooting and 21 points. Before Game 3, Smith had taken out a magic marker and written "2Ws" on his sneakers.

"There's room on the bandwagon, but either stay on or don't get on at all," Smith said. "If you want to jump on now, that's great. But don't jump off this time. A lot of people counted us out, but we wouldn't succumb to their criticism. We knew the big picture was the race to four wins."

Olajuwon said it was the media which fanned the flames of temporary discontent, not the fans.

"They wrote 'Choke City' and that showed their ignorance," Olajuwon said. "This is a seven-game series, and they were acting like it was over after two games. Labeling us 'Choke City' is bringing us closer as a team."

Who knows? Maybe those Houston headline writers will turn out to be the MVPs of this wacky series.

May 16

This is the neat thing about sports: The myriad of emotions, the ups and downs, the ecstasy and the agony.

In the span of five days, Houston fans have gone from one end of the spectrum to the other. The Rockets left town cast as bums and returned cast as gutsy, never-say-die heroes. As the Rockets charter airplane taxied in to Hobby Airport last night, the pilot called Rudy into the cockpit and explained there was a little problem.

But actually, that "problem" represented a happy resolution to Fan Flap. About 5,000 fans had turned out to welcome the Rockets home.

"I looked out the window and saw all of those people," Tomjanovich said. "There were so many of them. It was the greatest feeling."

It's amazing how this script has been altered.

The fans are welcoming the Rockets back. And the Suns are wondering about Barkley's back.

Sir Charles missed 27 of 43 shots in the weekend set of games. In Game 4, he failed to read Houston's rotating defense, throwing four interceptions while in an isolation position.

The Barkley hero worshippers insist he's hurting. Excuse me for being a bit cynical, but I didn't see any evidence of Barkley back pain when the Suns were winning Games 1 and 2. Barkley was jumping around, twisting in the air and laughing his way through each Suns comeback.

But now that Barkley has had two poor games and the Suns have lost twice, the back suddenly becomes *the* issue.

From the Phoenix perspective, it's as though Barkley couldn't possibly have a bad game unless his back is the problem. But maybe the real problem is the defense applied by Thorpe and Herrera.

The Suns' biggest ally now is twisted logic. Phoenix Coach Paul Westphal claims the Suns are in the driver's seat because they are on the *road.*

The Rockets, however, think it's time for the true home-court advantage to manifest itself because Houston has hit its stride.

"Offensively, from a shooting standpoint, the Suns may have more talent than us," Elie said. "But we're the better defensive team, and defense should prevail in a long series.

"Plus, we've adjusted offensively as this series has gone on. We didn't attack and stay aggressive in the first two games. But then we went to Phoenix and added the penetration aspect to our game.

"Right now, we feel good about what we're doing offensively and defensively. We've got a good feeling as a team, and we're getting stronger and stronger as this series goes on. I see no reason why that shouldn't continue."

The Rockets are beginning to get consistent bench production from Elie and Cassell. The rookie has come a long way since his playoff indoctrination against the Blazers, and Elie is in sync after overcoming the fractured hand injury and subsequent layoff.

Meanwhile, Maxwell has been taking Dan Majerle right out of the series. Majerle is in a terrible shooting slump and doesn't have the quickness to stop Maxwell's dribble penetration.

"The difference between the first two games and the last two games is that we've become aggressive," Smith said. "Walt Frazier used to say the regular season makes your name and the playoffs make your fame. If we stay aggressive like we've been in the last two games, maybe we'll all be famous."

Need more words of inspiration?

Olajuwon sat down in a courtside seat after today's practice and sounded his most optimistic note of the year.

"This is the best chance to win a championship that any Rockets team has had since I've played for," he said. "Everything is there for us. Home-court advantage the rest of the playoffs. Everything.

"We can win it all. But we must not panic . . . and we need the fans to give us a boost, not boo us. We need them to cheer us if it looks like we need a lift.

"I feel it . . . a championship. This is reality in front of us. Not something we *might* be able to do. It's something we *can* do if we keep our focus, our intensity, our feeling for one another."

It's the year of The Dream. If he believes it, all of Houston should.

May 17

Well, so much for that "home-court *dis*-advantage" theory.

On a night when some of the nervous Houston fans were worrying about a choke, the Rockets turned the Suns into a joke. Houston struck like a thunderbolt, built a 32-point cushion and won 109–86 to take a 3–2 series lead.

Looks like the Rockets have learned their lesson. When they got up by 20, they weren't content to tread water. They waded through the Suns to go ahead by 30.

"After Game 1, we sensed it," Smith said. "After Game 2, we knew it. The key against this Phoenix team is staying aggressive the whole game."

The Rockets led by 21 at the half, but Houston was obsessed with pushing the pedal to the metal. Those scars from the infamous Game 2 haven't been forgotten.

"I'll admit I had a few flashbacks," Horry said. "But we stayed on the attack in the third quarter and kept hitting our shots."

In less than a week, the Rockets have gone from the pits to the heights. They are one victory away from a date in the Western Conference Finals against either Denver or Utah.

This time, Barkley got his 30 points, but the rest of the Suns were dormant. Majerle went from bad to worse, missing all six of his shots. K.J.? After averaging 38 points in Games 3 and 4, the All-Star point guard was held to 4-of-13 shooting and just 10 points and two assists.

"We've gone from the penthouse to the poorhouse, but we'll show up Thursday," Barkley said. "They don't give you the series because you won one game by a lot of points. I'd rather get blown out than lose a close one."

One discouraging note for Houston: Herrera suffered a dislocated right shoulder in the second quarter and likely will miss the remainder of the series.

"We had a good defensive rotation going there with Thorpe and Herrera on Barkley," Tomjanovich said. "We'll have to look at all the options and make a decision."

Even without Herrera, the Rockets think they can wrap it up in six.

In the last 10 quarters, Houston has outscored the Suns 293–216 and outshot them 57.7 percent to 39.6.

As soon as they showered and finished interviews, the Rockets headed for Hobby Airport.

After Game 2, the late night Houston-to-Phoenix journey must have seemed interminable. Tonight, the Rockets are so keyed up they probably believe they could fly to Phoenix without an airplane.

What a weird business.

May 18

Joe Gilmartin, the longtime basketball pundit from the *Phoenix Gazette,* still believes the Suns will take this series and ultimately win the world championship.

Gilmartin has a sound theory to support his contention.

"You can win a championship without a great center," Gilmartin said. "But you can't win one without a great guard."

Gilmartin makes a valid point. Every championship team since I started covering the league in '79–'80 has had at least one blue-chipper in the backcourt. The list includes Magic Johnson (five titles), Isiah Thomas (two titles), Michael Jordan (three titles), Dennis Johnson (two titles), Maurice Cheeks (one title) and Nate "Tiny" Archibald (one title).

If you follow that line of thinking, it would seem that this is Kevin Johnson's year.

But there's something else to consider: All of the aforementioned championship teams were strong at the defensive end of the floor. Phoenix isn't, at least not on a consistent basis.

The Rockets are running rings around the Suns. Take away the Game 1 fatigue and the Game 2 fourth-quarter freeze and Houston's offense would be off the charts right now.

Nobody has said anything about it, but the Suns miss the athleticism of Richard Dumas. In the Suns' drive to the Western Conference championship last year, Dumas was a big part of the equation.

But substance abuse problems have prevented Dumas from playing this season.

Today, the Suns were all business. The bulk of the team refused to talk to the media. Johnson and Ainge were sent out as sacrificial lambs during the interview availability session.

"We want to practice," Johnson said. "We don't want to talk. No offense to you guys, but this is no time to be humorous or worry about flair."

Barkley wouldn't shut up during the first two games in Houston. But his comments grew shorter and less funny as the Rockets began to assert themselves. This may be Houston's greatest achievement yet: Zipping the lip of Sir Charles.

"All we want to do is get this series back to Houston," Johnson said. "In a one-game situation, we'll take our chances."

If the Rockets win tomorrow, I'm going to remind Gilmartin that his "great guard/championship" theory is on the rocks, even though Utah's John Stockton is still playing.

You might have to say it ain't so, Joe.

May 19

The Rockets are on the verge of doing something that hasn't been done in a quarter of a century. The last team to lose the opening two playoff games at home and come back to win a seven-game series was the 1969 Los Angeles Lakers.

That club, headed by Jerry West, Wilt Chamberlain and Elgin Baylor, dropped the opening two games at The Forum before winning four in a row against the San Francisco Warriors. The *Arizona Republic* had a story about that Lakers-Warriors series, and I was leisurely reading all about it this morning in my room when a siren sounded at the Ritz Carlton.

Moments later, somebody came on the hotel intercom with instructions for all guests to leave their rooms, avoid the elevators and file down the steps until they reached the lobby. My first thought was this had to be a fire alarm.

But as we marched quietly through the lobby and continued outside, under a piercing Arizona sun, one of the guests whispered there had been a bomb scare.

A canopy had been set up outside the hotel, with refreshments and plenty of chairs and tables. A hotel spokesman grabbed a microphone and confirmed there had been a telephone threat of a bomb. The hotel was being searched and guests were informed the wait would be about 90 minutes.

The Rockets' team bus was just leaving for the morning shootaround when the siren went off.

"I saw the people coming outside, but I thought it was just a convention letting out," Tomjanovich would later say.

Many of the guests were speculating that the bomb threat may have come from someone trying to distract the Rockets, but hotel officials wouldn't confirm that speculation.

By the time the Rockets got back from practice, guests had been allowed to return to their rooms. So, if indeed somebody had been trying to distract the Rockets, they failed.

The Suns, however, did not fail.

Phoenix controlled Game 6 thanks to its best defensive effort of the series and an offensive explosion by veteran A.C. Green, who responded to his promotion from sixth man to starter in a big way. In 37 ultra-productive minutes, Green hit 9 of 10 shots and finished with 22 points and 10 rebounds. Center Joe Kleine also gave the Suns a surprise boost by hitting some face-up jumpers when Olajuwon chose to hang close to the basket. Kleine had 15 points in just 27 minutes, and the Suns won 103–89.

So, after six games of thrills and spills, the Rockets and Suns are right back where they started on Mother's Day.

"Phoenix played a hell of a game, which you would expect," Tomjanovich said. "I was disappointed in our approach to the game. I think we could have made them work harder."

The whole evening was a horror show for Houston. Thorpe suffered a hip pointer early in the game and could not extend properly. Maxwell, Smith and Cassell were a combined 8 of 31 from the floor, and the Suns were able to capitalize on many of the Rockets long-range misses with open-floor opportunities.

"One game," Barkley said. "We'll show up in Houston and see what happens. All the world owes you is an opportunity."

Maxwell was ejected late in the game, and there was some commotion in the runway as he was being escorted to the locker room.

A driver for a television satellite truck allegedly taunted Maxwell, and Maxwell made a move toward the heckler before being restrained by Rockets officials and security personnel.

But Maxwell was cool, calm and confident after showering and putting on his street clothes.

Maxwell declared the Rockets will take Game 7. No ifs, ands or buts. "We're going to win the ballgame," Maxwell said. "Definitely."

There you have it. Mad Max guaranteed, but no money back.

May 20

I took the early-bird flight out of Phoenix and was waiting at Hobby when the respective charters of the Suns and Rockets landed within 30 minutes of each other.

This is it. Tomorrow's High Noon showdown at The Summit will decide this zany series once and for all. The Suns had it . . . then the Rockets had it . . . now, who really knows?

The Suns certainly know how to handle the pressure of a one-game season. They staved off elimination five times in last year's romp to The Finals. The Rockets were in two make-or-break games last year, winning a decisive Game 5 against the Clippers and losing the Game 7 overtime crusher in Seattle.

The winner moves into serious world championship contention. The loser may well be the second-best team in basketball but will be forced to watch the last month of the playoffs on television.

"Everybody's nervous," Barkley said. "Nobody's going to sleep tonight. Nobody's going to be hungry at dinner. My stomach hurts. My head hurts. Everybody tries to tell you a lie, but it's intense.

"I don't care how long you've been in the league. It gets harder. It's unbelievable mental anguish. Once you get to the tip-off, it's great."

I looked at the faces of the Rockets as they filed off the airplane and scurried for their cars. I didn't detect any fear or panic.

I really think the Rockets are immune to pressure right now. Pressure is going to Phoenix down 0–2 after the biggest fourth-quarter collapse in playoff history. If somebody would have told the Rockets at that point they could have one game—at home—to win this remarkable series, they would have been doing cartwheels in their hotel rooms.

Besides, history is on the Rockets' side. Since 1982 when Philadelphia won at Boston, the home team has gone 15–0 in Game 7s.

Houston has already gone through hell. This is Game 7 heaven.

May 21

It's over, and all I can say is that this Rockets-Suns series will be remembered as a fairy-tale script. Choke City was almost mystically transformed into Clutch City, with none other than Hakeem Olajuwon dutifully serving as the honorary mayor.

Rockets 104, Suns 94. All that preseason and regular-season work—all the pushing and prodding and sacrifice—paid off today. The Rockets labored long and hard to have Game 7 at home, and the reward was a victory that suddenly brings a once-blurry championship dream into sharp focus.

The Suns were valiant in defeat. But the Rockets used a lot of the old and a lot of the new to keep their season alive.

Olajuwon scored 23 of his 37 points in the second half to keep the Rockets in gear. Still, Houston wouldn't have won without an amazing performance by the rookie Cassell. He finished with 22 points and seven assists while playing with poise beyond his years.

With 4:50 remaining and the Rockets up by five, trouble was looming. The Suns were playing maniacal defense, and it looked like the shot clock was going to expire. Just before it did, Cassell reared up for a three-pointer.

Swish! Westphal could only produce a silly grin, turn his back to the court, spread his arms and look to the heavens. The picture was indeed worth a thousand words. Who the hell is this Cassell? That's what Westphal was saying with his body language.

The irony was that former NBA Coach Dick Versace happened to be working the game for national radio. After last year's draft, Versace had given the Rockets a "D-plus" for drafting Cassell. Hey, Dick, ready to change that grade?

"The media counted us out, but we never counted ourselves out," said a smiling Olajuwon. "I hope the media learned something from this series."

Even those in Journalism 101 will have to conclude this Rockets team has more character than characters. Houston had to beat an outstanding Phoenix club four out of five to move to the Western Conference Finals. Somehow, some way, the Rockets did it.

"We just got beat by a great team," Ainge said. "They outplayed us fair and square."

It was a sad, ugly ending for Barkley, who limped through the game with back and groin ailments.

With the Rockets in control in the final seconds, Barkley shoved a driving Olajuwon while Olajuwon's body was in midflight and vulnerable to injury. Barkley was ejected and left the court muttering obscenities at official Dick Bavetta.

"They shouldn't have tried to score again," Barkley said. "We had conceded the game. You don't rub it in when you've got the game won. That's why Ainge popped them in the head (in Game 3)."

The Suns will no doubt look back at this series and wonder how Majerle could have fallen so far, so fast. Majerle went 5 of 15 in Game 3; 2 of 10 in Game 4; 0 for 6 in Game 5; 1 for 7 in Game 6; and 3 of 11 in Game 7.

Houston's defensive scheme was outstanding. The Rockets mixed up their coverages and generally forced Barkley—a good but not great jump shooter—to prove himself from the perimeter. Rather than selling out with early double-teams on Barkley, the Rockets instructed Maxwell to stay at home against Majerle. Once Majerle's confidence waned, the big guard's shooting dilemma began to snowball.

Houston came down the stretch of Game 7 with perhaps its five toughest warriors on the floor: Olajuwon, Cassell, Horry, Elie and Maxwell. Instead of a choke, the Rockets applied the choke hold.

When the final buzzer sounded, the hallway leading to the Rockets locker room began to fill with happy well-wishers. I ran into Hall of Famer Elvin Hayes, who predicted Houston will go on to win it all.

As I was talking to Hayes, joyous Rockets minority owner Gary Bradley came along and—much to my surprise and chagrin—planted a wet kiss on my cheek.

Gary, please, control yourself.

The road to the world championship may go through Houston, but it's too early for smooching.

May 22

Well, I guess it was bound to happen sooner or later.

Gene Peterson hasn't exactly been Darell Garretson's most ardent supporter the last few years. Peterson thinks Garretson is past his prime as an official, and I've heard him express that opinion many times.

Garretson, who is in his last year as an active official, must have been getting some Geno feedback. While working Game 7 of the Suns-Rockets series, Garretson came over to press row yesterday and interrupted Peterson's broadcast with an editorial comment that went out over the airwaves.

"You're an asshole," Garretson shouted into the microphone.

Geno didn't miss a beat.

"We'll be back after these messages," Peterson said.

Ah, the joys of live radio. When in doubt, cut to a commercial.

Peterson and Garretson may have an opportunity to discuss anatomy lessons again as the playoffs roll along.

The Rockets have drawn Utah in the Western Conference Finals, and that means Houston must find a way to neutralize the imposing duo of Stockton and Malone.

"They are where they are because they've got two of the best players in the game who've played together for years," Rockets Assistant Coach Carroll Dawson said as Houston hurriedly put in its Utah game plan.

"It's an outstanding combination. You have to go way back in NBA history to find guys who played that well together. They know each other so well. It's instinct."

In each round of the Western Conference playoffs, there have been superstars yearning for a championship. First, Olajuwon and Drexler. Then Olajuwon and Barkley. Now, Olajuwon and Malone.

The Rockets will have the same sort of advantage tomorrow that Phoenix had in Game 1 of the last series. Utah is having to fly in today while the Rockets practice at home in a normal routine. It's similar to when the Rockets had to fly home from Portland with the Suns here waiting on them.

The Jazz won't have the firepower of Phoenix, but the Utah half-court defense figures to be tougher than the Suns' defense, with 300-pound Felton Spencer banging on Olajuwon.

Whereas the Suns liked to play fast, Utah will try to use a methodical tempo.

"We can play slow, fast or in between," Smith said. "Our records can play on 33 rpms or 45 rpms."

May 23

I know this world championship quest is getting serious because the Rockets are playing on my birthday. It's only the second time in 15 years of Rockets duty this has happened.

Hey, if tonight's opener against Utah is any indication, this Houston team may still be playing during Wimbledon.

The Rockets picked up where they left off against Phoenix while the Jazz looked as though it had a serious case of Mutombo hangover. In a 100–88 victory, Houston was sharper, quicker and better.

The Rockets had a devastating 1–2 punch in Olajuwon and Smith and were never seriously pushed after opening a 20-point halftime lead.

"The Rockets were terrific tonight," Utah Coach Jerry Sloan said. "They've got their eyes set on something bigger than us."

If that sounds like a concession speech, don't be fooled. The Jazz are notorious for looking bad in Game 1 but turning it around in Game 2. For Exhibit A, check the Utah-San Antonio series.

Utah simply didn't have the necessary energy level tonight, but Tomjanovich knows the Jazz will come back strong in Game 2.

"We know how tough it is to come back from a western time zone to play a team that's waiting on you," Tomjanovich said. "We felt this would be the game in which Utah had the least amount of fuel in its tank."

The Stockton-Smith matchup was supposed to heavily favor the Jazz. But when Stockton kept roaming away from his man in search of steals, Smith took advantage of the open looks to sink six shots from three-point range.

"If I get 10 open looks from the three-point line, I feel I'll hit seven of them," Smith said. "Whether it's 8 a.m. or 8 p.m."

It was a happy night all the way around for the Rockets, as official word began to circulate that Olajuwon will be named MVP at a news conference tomorrow.

Olajuwon will be Houston's first MVP since Moses Malone in 1982. The Dream finished the regular season ranked second in blocks (3.71), third in scoring (27.3), fourth in rebounding (11.9) and 10th in field-goal percentage (.528).

It's a perfect scenario.

Had the Rockets lost on Saturday to Phoenix, Olajuwon would have been accepting this award on a down note. I'm sure it wouldn't have had the same meaning to him if Houston had bowed out in the second round. But as it turned out, Olajuwon will be able to clutch the trophy while the national media is gathered in Houston to watch the Rockets in the conference finals.

Olajuwon has long said the MVP award is simply a byproduct of winning, and that notion will be reinforced tomorrow.

These days, the Rockets are truly living in Dreamland.

May 24

The Houston Post is going all out for tomorrow's Olajuwon MVP section, and I've been thinking a lot about what I want to say in my commentary.

I can't tell the fans anything about Olajuwon's game that they don't already know. The guy is great. Period.

Instead, I will try to give some perspective, some insight, into how Olajuwon's rise to become a Most Valuable Player parallels his rise to become a Most Valuable Person. This is a theme that has been forming in my mind all season.

I think back to an Olajuwon story told to me by former Rockets Coach Bill Fitch. On a fall day in 1984, the Olajuwon era started with a preseason trip to San Antonio. Five minutes after the team checked into its hotel, the telephone rang in Fitch's room:

"Coach, this is Akeem," Olajuwon said in slow, broken English.

"Yes, Akeem?"

"Coach, can you tell me how . . . do we go . . . to the game?"

The thought flashed through Fitch's mind that he truly was starting from scratch with this rookie who was just a few years removed from his Nigerian homeland.

"Akeem, we're going to the game on a bus," Fitch said gently.

It was then Fitch realized something had been lost in translation. What Olajuwon really wanted to know was what he should *wear* to the game.

Fitch provided the dress code information and the conversation ended shortly thereafter.

There's a reason why that vignette sticks in my mind. To know Olajuwon now—to observe daily how confident and comfortable he is in this crazy profession called the NBA—it seems incredulous that it all began with a question born of pure innocence.

Roll the tape fast-forward, please. That age of innocence has long since passed.

As a 21-year-old kid, Olajuwon began to learn how to go to the game. As a 31-year-old man blessed with a unique wisdom about life, he most definitely has learned not only how to go but what to do when he gets there.

So much has happened to Olajuwon since that fall day nearly 10 years ago when he started from ground zero.

There was the shy, naive introduction to the NBA in 1985 and 1986. There were the immature, temperamental years in the late 1980s and early 1990s when Olajuwon always seemed to be the eye of the storm as the Rockets floundered in mediocrity.

And then there was the spiritual awakening, the return to his Muslim beliefs and the ensuing tranquility and joy we now see on a day-to-day basis.

"Religion is to show your gratitude for all your blessings," Olajuwon said. "You are blessed just to be able to play the game. When you see the handicapped . . . blind people . . . you are just fortunate enough to have the athletic ability to play the game.

"You enjoy the worldly, but you don't attach yourself. You strive to follow a higher moral code. So, you show gratitude. Live the best way of life, which is very clean. To me, there's no other choice."

Traveling around the country with Olajuwon, I see him back up these words with deeds.

On commercial trips, he generally does not sit in first class. He prefers the extra leg room of the coach class bulkhead seat. There, he usually sits beside a star-struck fan rather than a teammate.

Almost without fail, Olajuwon becomes engrossed in a friendly conversation with the person seated next to him by the time the plane levels off. He loves to talk about a variety of subjects: Art, fashion, religion, philosophy, business and, yes, even sports.

He is respectful and polite, never putting on airs as though he's better than the man, woman, girl or boy seated next to him.

I see the Most Valuable Person traits during the Rockets leisure time on the road. While some players are scanning the box scores, Olajuwon reads from the Koran, the sacred book of Islam.

I see the Most Valuable Person traits in his disciplined lifestyle. He speaks often about the importance of eating the right foods and getting plenty of rest.

I see the Most Valuable Person traits when the lights come on and players who don't have Olajuwon's skill level often try to compensate with violent behavior and cheap-shot antics.

These days, nothing flusters Olajuwon. He laughs, he smiles, he enjoys the competition.

Before he rededicated himself to his Muslim religion, Olajuwon was obsessed with winning a championship. He feared it would never happen in Houston.

"That is my biggest problem," he once told me.

Olajuwon wouldn't say such a thing now, of course. Certainly, he wants to win a title, but he has come to understand there are more important things in the grand scheme of life. The irony is that as his priorities have come into focus, so has the vision of a championship ring.

That's all part of the awakening of a Most Valuable Person.

Tomorrow, NBA Commissioner David Stern will hand Olajuwon an MVP trophy, signifying that—for this year, at least—he is the No. 1 basketball player in the world.

But the jump shots, the hook shots and the blocked shots aren't as impressive to me as the manner in which Olajuwon has adjusted his way of life in the last couple of years.

Nice guys *can* finish first, and Olajuwon ranks as a shining example.

This Most Valuable Person learned how to go to the game. He's taking all of Houston along for the joyous ride.

In typical dramatic fashion, Olajuwon went out tonight and made the MVP voters look like the smartest people in America.

I had figured maybe the big guy would have a bit of an emotional letdown after all the pomp and ceremony regarding the MVP announcement. Olajuwon had been eulogized in the Houston media to such a degree that a Salt Lake columnist, Lee Benson, wryly wondered whether Olajuwon checked to see if he was alive when he arrived at the arena.

No way Olajuwon could live up to the mega-hype, right? Wrong.

The Houston center capped his MVP day with a memorable shootout against the gallant Malone. When the smoke cleared, Olajuwon was standing tall with a 41-point, 13-rebound work sheet. Only the individual brilliance of Olajuwon enabled Houston to win 104–99 and take a 2–0 lead in the Western Conference Finals.

"Nobody was going to spoil the MVP's night," Smith said. "Karl Malone is very, very good. But Hakeem is a cut above everybody else."

As expected, the Jazz roared back from its Game 1 debacle to play a brilliant Game 2. But Olajuwon simply wouldn't let Houston lose. On eight consecutive possessions down the stretch, Olajuwon and Malone traded scores.

Classic. It was like watching two great gunslingers in a top-rated western shooting it out on Main Street.

With Houston up 98–97 and 39 seconds remaining, Olajuwon provided the *coup de grace* with an improbable running bank shot going left to right across the lane.

Olajuwon landed on the seat of his pants, and the ball landed in the bottom of the net. That score drained the final bit of energy from a Utah team that had done its best to be MVP party poopers.

"I was just playing to win," Olajuwon said when his banner night was over. "That's how I got MVP . . . by striving for team success and doing whatever I could do to help my team."

Sounds simple. It wasn't.

This was the game Utah believed it could steal. But in the end, the Jazz couldn't cope with the will and the skill of Olajuwon. Years from now, when we look back on Hakeem the Legend, I have a feeling this performance will come to the forefront.

Before tip-off, Olajuwon had sent chills down Tomjanovich's spine by asking the entire team and coaching staff to help accept the MVP trophy from Stern.

"Basketball is a team sport," Olajuwon explained. "The MVP trophy belongs to the whole team."

That's true. But within the confines of this team sport, one player must be a constant source of strength if there is to be a championship parade.

"For Hakeem to have had this type of game on the night he received the MVP trophy . . . rarely do things fit together like that," Tomjanovich said.

In addition to the Olajuwon heroics, Elie played a big role in the victory. He came off the bench for 17 points and hit a clutch three-pointer to break a 93–93 tie at the 1:55 mark.

It's on to Utah, where the Jazz will almost certainly have to win Games 3 and 4 to advance to The Finals. On the flight home, Utah will no doubt think about how close it came to changing the entire complexion of this series in Game 2.

Too much Hakeem.

What Magic Johnson did for the Lakers, what Michael Jordan did for the Bulls, what Larry Bird did for the Celtics . . . that's what Olajuwon is doing for the Rockets.

May 26

From my room at the Salt Lake Marriott, I can see, among other things, the Mormon Tabernacle and the snow-capped Wasatch mountain range. Everything seems serene around here, but I'm not sure that's the case at Jazz headquarters.

Last week, in Game 5 of the Utah-Denver series, tempestuous Jazz owner Larry Miller had made a fool of himself. After Malone missed his first seven shots, Miller stood on the baseline and screamed for Sloan to bench the Mailman.

I'm not sure who Miller had in mind as a replacement for the best power forward in the league. Luther Wright, maybe?

For an owner to upstage his highly competent coach and best player in this manner is reproachable. They say the incident has been smoothed over, but I have to wonder if it didn't at least subconsciously affect the karma of this ballclub.

Utah is a small-market team. Its success over the last decade has revolved around the family atmosphere of the town and the organization. It has been a one-for-all and all-for-one environment.

How can Malone ever feel the same about this organization after what Miller did to him? And how must the other Jazz players feel, knowing the owner has publicly ridiculed the main man in such a classless fashion?

I'm not saying the Jazz will roll over and play dead. Far from it, as evidenced by Game 2. I'm just saying the Miller tirade might have created an overall unsettling atmosphere at a crucial juncture in the season.

At any rate, that's Utah's problem. Houston's problem is fighting human nature. With a 2–0 series lead, the Rockets won't be in a must-win situation tomorrow. Their *modus operandi* is a road split.

But if the Rockets let up . . . well, remember the Phoenix series. Once the momentum turns, anything is possible.

Tomjanovich is imploring his team to go for the jugular in Game 3. This is a "What have you done for me lately?" kind of business.

May 27

Put those brooms back in the closet. So much for the lofty dreams of a Rockets sweep.

In the comfort of the raucous Delta Center, Utah joined the fight in convincing fashion. The Jazz held Olajuwon to 0 for 8 shooting early in the game and went on to a 95–86 victory that narrowed Houston's series lead to 2–1.

From a Rockets' perspective, this one could only be described as an ugly, frustrating affair.

Houston got on the refs' bad side by picking up four—count 'em—four technicals in the first half. On a night when they needed 48 minutes of skill and composure, the Rockets had neither.

"We beat ourselves in three areas," Smith said. "We didn't swing the ball for open shots, we didn't get back defensively and we got involved with the referees."

All I can say is, it's a good thing Houston pulled out Game 2 thanks to Olajuwon's herculean effort. Otherwise, the Jazz would be up 2–1 and in a position to win Game 4 at home and take a commanding lead in the series.

Then again, maybe Houston would have played better if it had come into Game 3 feeling threatened.

We're seeing a pattern here. The Rockets go to Portland leading 2–0 and don't play well. They go to Phoenix for Game 6 leading 3–2 and don't play well. Now, they've come into Utah leading 2–0 and unraveled before our eyes.

To have the energy and adrenaline to excel in road playoff competition, I'm getting the idea this Houston team has to believe it is backed into a corner.

The Rockets didn't have "the edge" because they didn't feel an urgency to win Game 3. This is what Rudy means when he talks about fighting human nature.

"This game was similar to our Game 3 at Portland," Tomjanovich said. "We said all the right things, but we didn't execute and we didn't have the energy level that Utah showed."

At the outset, Olajuwon had trouble adjusting to Salt Lake's 4,500-foot altitude. He couldn't get his wind. Thus, the 0 of 8 start.

News flash: Hakeem is human.

"When you get tired, you don't have the energy to fight back for position," Olajuwon said. "I know it because the same thing happened to me in Denver."

The Jazz received timely offensive performances from David Benoit, an athletic small forward, and veteran guard Jay Humphries. But it was Houston's lackluster .359 field-goal percentage that put Utah back in the series.

"Tough night," said Elie, who symbolized Houston's plight with his 0 for 7 shooting in 21 minutes. "We got our butts kicked tonight. But we're still extremely confident. We'll be ready for Game 4."

May 28

Coming back from dinner tonight, I bumped into Hakeem in the hotel elevator. He had been watching a local sportscast.

"They're giving Spencer credit for stopping me," Olajuwon said.

Hakeem didn't elaborate, but it was obvious he questioned the validity of that report.

Having adjusted to the altitude, I've got to believe Hakeem will be in a high-energy mode tomorrow. His teammates figure to be ready, too.

Since the Game 2 debacle against Phoenix, the Rockets have not lost two playoff games in a row. After each defeat, they have bounced back with a vengeance.

"We had a very easy Game 1, but then they came back hard the second time," Olajuwon had said after today's practice. "Now, it's our second road game, and we know what must be done."

Indeed, this could be the game that gives Houston a firm springboard to the championship round.

"If we win, we're in great shape at 3–1," Smith said. "If we lose, we're right back where we started a week ago."

Malone missed today's Utah practice because of the flu. But he'll be there for the matinee tip-off.

It would probably take double pneumonia to keep the Mailman out of Game 4.

At this stage of the season, you leave whatever you've got on the court.

May 29

The superstars were upstaged today. Olajuwon, Malone and Stockton are the marquee names in this series, but they had to step aside so Utah timekeeper Wayne Hicken could contribute to the NBA's all-time blooper reel.

Hicken has become my hero. Here's a man who truly can make time stand still.

The Rockets won 80–78, but not before Hicken embellished a wild ending by freezing at crunch time. With Houston leading by two points and 13.5 seconds remaining, Hicken failed to start the clock for about nine seconds after the Jazz had thrown the ball inbounds.

Finally, Tom Chambers missed a shot, and Horry made a spectacular dive over two Utah players to collect the rebound from a prone position. At that point, the Rockets got a break. Utah didn't attack Horry because the instincts of the Jazz players told them the game should be over.

With Utah confused and hesitant, Horry alertly flipped the ball to a teammate, allowing the Rockets to race down the floor and *finally* run out the clock.

The press row scene was hilarious.

From my seat, I could hear Peterson going bonkers because the timekeeper was asleep at the switch. His sidekick, Foley, was yelling, too. This caught the attention of official Jess Kersey, who wound up in a heated conversation with Foley.

"I used to respect you guys," Kersey said.

Meanwhile, a crestfallen Hicken quickly left the arena after saying "I got caught up in the game."

I'm convinced there was no malice of forethought on Hicken's part. He is a Jazz fan, naturally, and simply became transfixed while hoping his team would score a basket and force overtime.

Bill Worrell had the best line of the day, telling *The Houston Post*'s Kenny Hand: "If I ever get the electric chair, I want to fly this guy in to work the switch."

Poor Wayne. He never would have been become the butt of the time-clock jokes if the Rockets had played with any degree of intelligence down the stretch. Houston put forth a gutsy defensive effort all day, and the offense was boosted by Smith's 25 points. With a minute to go, Houston had the ball and a seven-point lead. That's when serious brainlock set in.

The Rockets then made every junior-high mistake in the book, and the follies show culminated with Cassell blatantly pushing aside Stockton for an offensive foul that gave Utah the ball down 80–78 with 13.5 to go.

"It wasn't panic," Tomjanovich said. "It was dumbness."

In times of crisis this year, Houston's saving grace has been solid half-court defense. The Rockets needed one clean stop, and they got it—Hicken notwithstanding.

I'm not sure what would have happened if the Jazz had scored during the final bizarre sequence. I imagine all hell would have broken loose, with Hicken winding up as a national celebrity.

Jay Leno and David Letterman probably would have had a field day with this one.

But the Rockets prevailed and now figure to quickly wrap up this series at home.

Hicken?

He has the off-season to practice flipping the switch.

With Rockets' Fever getting hotter by the day, there's no time to have a life anymore.

If you're from Houston, the Rockets probably have become the center of your universe.

Those of us in the print media can't write enough about this team, and the radio and television coverage has become intense, too.

Anybody got a fresh angle?

On the flight home from Salt Lake today, I was thinking about how well Smith and Horry played yesterday.

Smith scored almost one-third of his team's 80 points, and Horry had a solid all-round effort with 11 points, 10 rebounds, five assists, three steals and a couple of blocks.

Smith and Horry. They represent the resiliency in the Rockets makeup.

There was a time during the winter when Kenny Bashing was such a popular sport it could have been included in the Lillehammer Olympics. There was a time during the winter when Horry found himself stuck in a Detroit hotel room, awaiting approval to suit up for the Pistons.

Smith and Horry. They figured they were in a doghouse built for two.

But because they showed resiliency, the starting point guard and starting small forward are now one victory away from the big show.

There are certain things Smith doesn't do well. There are certain things Horry doesn't do well. But when you add Smith's outside shooting and Horry's all-around athleticism into the Rockets equation, the result is team success.

"It is as though the rain has gone away and the fog has lifted," Smith said. "This team has gone through a process of finding its true identity. It wasn't clear before. But it is now."

The deeper the Rockets go into the playoffs, the more Horry is asked to relive The Trade That Wasn't.

During halftime of yesterday's game, NBC did a big feature on that topic.

"What's happening now really feels good," Horry said. "Things happen for a reason. I was traded, then I came back and now I have a chance to be on a team that goes to The Finals. I think this whole experience has made me better."

May 31

From the outset, there was never a doubt.

Thorpe converted a layup and it was 2–0. Maxwell stroked a three-pointer, 5–0. Maxwell again from long range . . . 8–0.

Timeout, Utah. If you missed the first minute, you missed the statement: The Houston Rockets *are* the best in the West.

Houston had a 24-point lead at the start of the fourth quarter and held off a late Utah flurry to win 94–83 and take the series 4–1.

From the lottery in 1992 to championship legitimacy in 1994 . . . that is the Rockets' special renaissance story. Houston is headed to The Finals for the third time in franchise history and, for the first time, it will be favored to claim the title.

"What a great feeling," Tomjanovich said. "I've been there (to The Finals) as a player, I've been there as an assistant coach. But this one is the best.

"These guys have worked hard for me for two years. I've been blessed to coach a team that works hard on defense and shares the ball on offense."

The environmental report in Clutch City keeps getting better and better. Could it be that long-suffering Houston sports fans are really on the verge of watching a world championship parade?

Yes, the Rockets went to The Finals in 1981 and 1986. But with a young Larry Bird in their path, nobody really expected the Rockets to win.

I was eager to go into the locker room tonight because I wanted to get a sense of whether the ballclub is totally focused on winning it all. Were the players going to stage a full-fledged celebration for just getting *to* The Finals? Or would the mood be more reserved because the final hurdle is yet to come?

I'm told there was a team prayer and then a brief initial celebration before the media came in. But not the wild, emotional outburst that I remember when Ralph Sampson sank the buzzer beater that lifted Houston into the 1986 Finals.

"This is like tasting the icing on the cake," Smith said. "Now, we want to eat the cake. I don't think any team in the world can beat us four of seven. Maybe four of 10, but not four of seven."

If Horry continues to play like a man possessed, New York or Indiana is going to be in trouble. This is definitely not the Horry we saw in January. The young man from Alabama is hitting the outside shot and turning into a powerful dunking machine. He's going to the basket with playoff-caliber force and may have had his best overall game of the year tonight.

In 34 whirlwind minutes, Horry had 22 points and nine rebounds. Think Sloan doesn't wish that Horry-for-Elliott trade had gone through?

"When Houston got Robert Horry, it made it very difficult for us to play them," Sloan said. "He was sensational in this one."

The Rockets are already thinking about their championship series opponent. Les Alexander said he hopes Houston plays New York in The Finals. Elie was chortling "New York, New York" after the game.

Olajuwon, however, said he had no rooting interest in the Eastern Conference Finals.

"I'm just so happy we have put ourselves in a position to win a championship," Olajuwon said. "The rest is destiny."

June 1

The Western Conference champions have been given a well-deserved day off. So, there's nothing for me to do today except kick back and examine in some detail how the West was won and how the city is dealing with it.

The Rockets have left a trail of agony in their path. Coach Rick Adelman and vice president of basketball operations Geoff Petrie no longer have jobs in Portland. The Suns' Barkley is trying to decide whether to retire, and Utah's Malone isn't sure he wants to play for the Jazz next year.

All the Western Conference joy is here in Houston, where Rockets' Fever is escalating into a happy epidemic. Whether Houstonians are standing on a street corner, sitting in a coffee shop or taking a dip in the neighborhood pool, there's a Rockets' conversation going on today somewhere in their vicinity.

Kids on my block who used to wear Chicago Bulls caps and shirts are suddenly wearing Rockets caps and shirts.

It's cool to be a Rockets fan these days. And this phenomenon is only going to become more pronounced as the countdown to the championship series begins.

Regardless of whether New York or Indiana comes out of the East, I'm going to pick the Rockets. The questions I had about this team going into the playoffs have been answered to my satisfaction.

Going into the Portland series, the bench was suspect. Elie came back just in time to make some meaningful contributions, and Cassell has grown up right before our eyes. Plus, it looks like Herrera will return from his dislocated shoulder injury in the title series.

Horry has been a revelation lately, and Thorpe has been rocky-steady in terms of doing the dirty work and guarding highly touted forwards such as Barkley and Malone.

Maxwell has had great defensive efforts against Majerle and Hornacek in the last two rounds and is always capable of exploding offensively. Smith? He came up huge in two of the four wins over Utah.

Then there's Olajuwon, who will get his championship if there is any justice in this league.

Olajuwon used the word "destiny" last night. I think he's on a date with destiny, like Jordan was when the Bulls won their first title in 1991.

Olajuwon is the Defensive Player of the Year and the Most Valuable Player. He has paid his dues through 10 years of meritorious NBA service.

How many more chances can there be for this future Hall of Famer? Hakeem turned 31 in January. If he doesn't win this year, who knows if this title series opportunity will come his way again?

The time is now. For Hakeem . . . and for all those Houston fans starving for a long-awaited pro sports title.

June 2

Good things seem to happen to the Rockets after they visit Galveston Island.

After a preseason training camp in Galveston, Houston produced a 15–0 start. After a playoff training camp in Galveston, the Rockets waded through the Western Conference competition to reach the NBA Finals.

With the Knicks and Pacers locked in a long series, the NBA has decreed Game 1 of the championship round won't begin until June 8. So, the Rockets are back in Galveston for yet another tuneup.

As I cruised south to the island city on Interstate 45 this morning, I was considering the pros and cons of the team having a week off this late in the season. On one hand, Houston will have plenty of time to rest the legs and get over a litany of nagging injuries. Herrera, recovering from a dislocated shoulder, will have the opportunity to prove in practice whether he's ready for Finals competition. Horry and Thorpe are nursing sore right hips. Maxwell has more aches and pains than an NFL quarterback on Monday mornings, and Olajuwon needs to refuel his energy tank.

The flip side is that the winner of the New York-Indiana series will be battle-hardened when the championship series commences.

Two or three days off would have been ideal. But eight days without a game? I'm not sure this layoff will be in Houston's best interest.

I checked into the Galvez Hotel and then headed out to the Texas A&M Mitchell Campus practice facility. When the session ended, some of the Rockets seemed disappointed about last night's Pacers-Knicks result.

Reggie Miller responded to filmmaker Spike Lee's taunts by shooting down New York at Madison Square Garden. Thus, Indiana leads the Eastern Conference Finals 3–2 and can wrap it up at Market Square Arena tomorrow night.

I understand the Rockets players' sentiment. An Indiana-Houston Final just wouldn't create the national appeal of a New York-Houston Final.

A lot of people don't seem to realize that over the second half of the season, the Pacers evolved into an outstanding team under Larry Brown. If the Rockets were to beat Indiana for the title, that accomplishment would draw a lot of yawns from a national perspective.

The Rockets want to do it against big, bad New York.

They believe this act belongs on Broadway.

June 3

Finals Fame is beginning to overtake Rudy T.

As he walked through the line at Luby's Cafeteria yesterday, it seemed there were more well-wishers than menu selections. Writers from around the country want to do Tomjanovich profiles these days, and the electronic media requests are staggering.

These are fast, giddy, wonderful times for the Rockets coach. He deserves every verbal bouquet thrown his way.

What a job this man has done since reluctantly taking the Rockets' head coaching job on Feb. 18, 1992. If Olajuwon is the Rockets' magic potion, Tomjanovich is the straw that stirs the drink.

Rudy has hit the jackpot with his draft choices. He has provided a system tailored to take advantages of the players' strengths. He has demonstrated an uncanny knack for making the right moves with an unconventional substitution pattern done "by feel."

Beyond that, Tomjanovich is the definitive "Mr. Rocket." He has been a company man for 24 years as a five-time All-Star player, scout, assistant coach and head coach. The shoemaker's son from Hamtramck, Mich., truly has deep feelings for this city and this organization.

You like to see good things happen to good people. Tomjanovich succeeds with acumen, honesty, loyalty, hard work and an ego that's about the size of a peanut.

If the Rockets win the championship, I hope the national perception of Tomjanovich will change. Ask a sports fan in Iowa about Tomjanovich today and the response probably will be: "Oh, isn't he the guy who had his face punched in by Kermit Washington?"

Should this Rockets team become world champions, Tomjanovich ought to be nationally known not for taking a punch in 1977, but for doing one of the all-time great coaching jobs from 1992 through 1994.

If anybody had suggested to me two years ago today that the lottery-stained Rockets would be in the '94 Finals, I would have filed the notion in the temporary insanity category.

But Tomjanovich has assembled the pieces and created a climate for success. This year, he had the added burden of running the basketball operation by himself in lieu of a general manager.

Rudy T. The 'T' stands for terrific.

In the Finals, Rudy will go against either Brown or Pat Riley. Both Brown and Riley are acclaimed as top-of-the-line in their profession.

The Rockets won't be out-coached in The Finals. I'm sure of that.

Maybe the Rockets will get their wish after all.

Last night, the Knicks came through with a gutsy effort in Indianapolis, forcing a Game 7 that will be played in New York. The Rockets coaching staff watched the game while dining in a private room at Mario's restaurant on the Seawall. A few members of the media stopped by to get a quick reaction.

"The longer a series goes, the less preparation time there is for the next opponent," Tomjanovich said. "Let the Knicks and Pacers think about each other for one more game. We just have to continue to get ourselves ready to face either team."

From all accounts, the Galveston minicamp has been successful. There was a brief scare the other day when Horry had a minor traffic accident while driving to Galveston. The brakes in his car malfunctioned on Highway 6, and Horry wound up hitting another vehicle. But there were no major injuries, and Horry has practiced the last couple of days.

Meanwhile, Herrera continues to make progress. He envisions himself playing in Game 1, but Tomjanovich wants to withhold judgment until he sees Herrera test his shoulder in a couple of full-contact scrimmages.

The last Galveston practice was held today, and the scene outside the gym was more interesting than what was going on inside.

At least 100 fans gathered under a broiling sun, in hopes that they would be able to get an autograph or two from their heroes.

Everybody loves a winner.

In late April, when we came here before the Portland series, the only person outside the gym was the security guard.

With all the adulation the Rockets are getting during this off-week, the issue has to be raised: Will Houston show up for Game 1 acting like hungry lions or fat cats?

"There has been a lot of disappointment in Houston pro sports and now people have an outlet—us," Smith said. "It's fun, but we can't lose focus about what's going on. We have to remember that reaching the championship series wasn't our goal. Our goal is to win it. And to do that, we have to be every bit as committed as we were in the previous rounds."

I asked Horry about the implications of Rockets' Fever, and his reply was that it creates both positives and negatives.

"Some people would like to go out and not be bothered as much," Horry said. "You lose some ability to just go out and have fun. But that type of enthusiasm is really going to work for us once we step on the court for Game 1. You need the crowd energy and the adrenaline lift that the fans provide."

The players were free to drive back to the city after practice.

Tomorrow, the championship foe will be identified. Since no home team has lost Game 7 since '82, it looks like Gotham City versus Clutch City is a strong possibility.

June 5

Somewhere, NBC executives must be shouting from the skyscrapers and exchanging high-fives.

The big-market Eastern Conference team is in and the small-market team is out. The Knicks climbed on Patrick Ewing's back tonight, and the New York big man carried his team into the NBA Finals.

With the Knicks down 12 points late in the third quarter, Ewing exerted his will and took over the game. Ewing finished with 24 points, 22 rebounds, seven assists and five blocked shots as the Knicks came on late for a 94–90 victory over the pesky Pacers.

Start spreading the news: It's the Rockets versus the Knicks; Olajuwon versus Ewing.

The Houston players were off today, but the coaching staff watched the game at The Summit and began breaking down the Knicks on videotape after the final buzzer. Tomjanovich came out of his office briefly to accommodate the media.

"When you are shooting hoops in the driveway as a kid, this is what you're dreaming about," Tomjanovich said.

Isn't that the same thought Rudy expressed when the Rockets went to New York with a 14–0 record on Dec. 2?

Oh well, it never hurts to recycle a good quote.

Tomjanovich saw the spirit of the Knicks in that rousing fourth-quarter comeback. The Pacers never gave in; the Knicks just took what they felt was rightfully theirs.

"That New York team is a lot like us," Tomjanovich said. "They have a lot of heart."

The Olajuwon-Ewing matchup will, of course, serve as the main attraction. In the Year of the Center, it seems fitting these two warriors should be in The Finals.

"That (center matchup) is good for the sport, but people also have to remember it's a *team* game," Tomjanovich said.

It's the Beasts of the East versus the Best of the West.

The hour was late, but Tomjanovich headed back into his office. He had work to do.

June 6

If you're a baby boomer, enjoy sports and have lived in Houston since the late 1970s, you probably remember the famous Bum Phillips speech.

The Oilers lost by two touchdowns to Pittsburgh in the 1979 AFC championship game. A crowd of 50,000 gathered at the Astrodome to welcome the team home, and Phillips thought the fans wanted to hear something positive after the Oilers had fallen one game short of the Super Bowl two years running.

"Last year, we knocked on the door," Phillips shouted. "This year, we banged on the door. Next year, we're gonna kick the son of a bitch in!"

What does this have to do with the Rockets?

A lot.

The problem is that 15 years have gone by since Bum's proclamation and the S.O.B. *still* hasn't been kicked in. Houston teams have been on the threshold of a championship several times, but no cigar and no champagne.

It has been a maddening journey that always results in bridesmaid pit stops: The '78 and '79 Oilers couldn't get past the powerful Steelers; the 1980 Astros had a three-run lead in the eighth inning of their decisive game against the Phillies in the National League championship series—with Nolan Ryan on the mound. Houston lost.

The 1981 and 1986 Rockets are the only Houston team in an established major-league sport to have reached the championship round. In each of those years, the Rockets got past Magic Johnson, but not Bird.

The 1986 Astros took a three-run lead into the ninth inning of Game 6 in the NLCS against New York. Had Houston won that game, it had the virtually unbeatable Mike Scott ready for Game 7. But the Astros couldn't hold that Game 6 cushion.

Even on the collegiate level, Houston seems jinxed. The University of Houston Cougars—led by Olajuwon—seemed a cinch to defeat Cinderella North Carolina State in the 1983 NCAA title game. The Cougars lost at the buzzer after blowing a big lead.

And then there was the 1984 Houston-Georgetown title game when Ewing's Hoyas whipped Olajuwon's Cougars.

Because of what has happened in this city's ill-fated sports background, the Rockets will either be heartthrobs or heartbreakers. They will either make dreamy history or cause sorrowful histrionics.

Some would call this pressure. Others would call it a golden opportunity.

"It's the city that never sleeps versus the city that never wins," the New York Times surmised.

If the Rockets become the first Houston team to win a world championship in an existing league, they will own this town forever.

June 7

The national and international media began pouring into town today. Pack journalism is officially under way at The Summit.

The growth of the NBA Finals as a media event is an amazing story. In 1981, when the Rockets made their first Finals appearance, there weren't many reporters outside of Boston and Houston staffing the series. Now, The Finals is covered by media members from all over the world.

With the championship series commencing tomorrow, Olajuwon and Ewing are understandably attracting much of the crowd.

There were so many media members surrounding the centers, I was working like Otis Thorpe to establish inside position so I could hear what was being said.

"It's a dream matchup," said Olajuwon. "You've got two centers who respect each other so much. In a championship setting. With the world watching. A classic."

Olajuwon. Ewing. Maybe bigger really *is* better.

This NBA Finals is going to be special for Wilt Chamberlain, Bill Russell, Kareem Abdul-Jabbar and George Mikan.

This NBA Finals will be special for those connoisseurs of pivot play who have waited more than a decade for the great big man to truly become a center of attention again.

Most of all, this NBA Finals will be special for Olajuwon and Ewing.

Memo to Larry Bird, Magic Johnson, Michael Jordan and Isiah Thomas: Goliath is back in championship vogue.

Not since 1983—when Philadelphia's Moses Malone joined forces with Julius Erving—has a dominant big man been the focal point of a title team. Sure, Robert Parish was outstanding on three championship teams in Boston and Abdul-Jabbar could still do significant damage in 1985 with the Showtime Lakers. But the spotlight in those years was on Bird and Johnson, respectively.

Whatever happened to the good old days when the center was No. 1 on a No. 1 team?

It's going to happen this year for either Olajuwon or Ewing. One great big man will walk away with a ring, perhaps ushering in an era when the center position again becomes the glamour spot in the aftermath of Bird, Johnson and Jordan.

"I respect Patrick's game tremendously," Olajuwon said. "He will battle you. He's tough, physically and mentally. And he's a winner. He hates to lose."

So does Olajuwon. But one of these great centers *must* lose.

I saw longtime NBA Coach Jack Ramsay—now an ESPN analyst—among the media throng today and asked him to rate the centers.

"I would give Hakeem the edge because he's quicker, more active and has a greater variety of shots," Ramsay said. "I would say Patrick is a little more powerful. Both centers have become good passers. There's a thin differential, but the advantage goes to Hakeem."

The Rockets don't think Ewing will be able to contain Olajuwon if the Knicks are reluctant to provide double-team help. Riley said today he isn't ruling out double teams but will be extremely selective in the defensive decisions.

"Hakeem is the best player in the world," Elie said. "The other guy (Jordan) plays baseball. New York will *have* to double down on Hakeem."

The Rockets haven't had a game in a week, but it seems more like a month.

Clearly, they are ready to stop talking and start playing.

I'm picking the Rockets in six because of their home-court advantage and an edge in athleticism. New York will counter with physical, kamikaze defense and tenacious offensive rebounding.

These teams have a lot of similarities. Besides the great center matchup, both clubs have a streak-shooting, trash-talking big guard. The Maxwell-John Starks confrontation should be exciting.

Thorpe and Charles Oakley will battle for blue-collar supremacy at power forward, and each bench is led by a former CBAer who made good. Houston's Elie came up the hard way and ditto for the Knicks' Anthony Mason.

Four wins until glory? Or four losses until misery?

The collective psyche of Houston sports fans hangs in the balance.

June 8

"Hellhole" 1, N.Y. 0.

The Houston Post was put to bed tonight with that emphatic front page headline.

New York Post columnist Wally Matthews pulled the oldest journalistic trick in the book yesterday by trashing the city of Houston and thereby stoking civic pride. Showing absolutely no appreciation for the virtues of humidity, Wally ripped Houston, prompting his newspaper to label the Bayou City a "hellhole."

I hear the mayor's office wants to know where he's staying.

"Hey, it was a joke," Matthews said in the Rockets' locker room before tip-off.

Hellhole, huh? Well, Wally, the Knicks certainly felt the heat tonight.

The Rockets looked rusty on offense after their eight-day layoff, but the defense carried them to an 85–78 victory. One down, three to go for a Houston title. But don't plan the parade route just yet.

Houston was stretched to the limit, scoring only 13 points in the final period. The Knicks, however, shot only .341 from the floor, with Starks' 3-of-18 shooting performance preventing New York from having any sustained scoring spurts.

"You've got to be able to step up and make shots," Riley said. "That's a universal disease of ours, or at least that's the perception."

Olajuwon got off to a quick start, scoring 19 points in the first half to stake Houston to a 54–46 lead. The Knicks did a much better job of contesting shots in the second half, but fine work by Thorpe and Herrera at the power forward spot kept Houston in front.

Thorpe finished with 14 points and 16 rebounds while Herrera came off the bench to hit 5 of 6 shots in his first appearance since Game 5 of the Phoenix series.

Obviously, "Amigo" is back to 100 percent. Coming back from a dislocated shoulder, he dislocated the Knicks.

There's something about the Knicks that brings out the best in Herrera. He had a career-high 15 rebounds at Madison Square Garden in December, and now he has provided just enough of an offensive spark off the bench to put Houston ahead in a title series for the first time in club history.

"I worked my butt off to get back," Herrera said.

The key play came with Houston holding a precarious 80–76 lead. Smith was able to make a rare penetration against New York's defense, and Ewing had to come off Thorpe to pick up the driver. Smith delivered a pass to Thorpe, who took one big step and slammed the ball home for a six-point lead at the 1:02 mark.

In short, Rockets rustiness defeated Knicks fatigue.

New York appeared mentally and physically drained after the exhausting series against Indiana. The Knicks aren't a great shooting team, but there's no way they are going to stay down in the 34 percent range.

I figure the Rockets' offense will flow better in Game 2, as well. Maxwell finished just 4 of 16, Horry was 3 of 10 and Smith got off only four shots, hitting one.

Besides the game and the "Hellhole" subplot, the other intriguing aspect tonight revolved around Knicks' super fan Spike Lee.

Yes, Spike got his courtside seat at The Summit after much furor about whether he would. Nobody is saying what he paid for the privilege, but five figures was the rumor.

Little Spike should have moved about 20 feet in from where he was sitting and hoisted a few three-pointers. He couldn't have done much worse than Starks and Derek Harper, who finished 3 of 10.

Draw no conclusions, though.

This is probably going to be a repeat of what the Rockets went through early in the Utah series. The Jazz shot miserably in Game 1 but bounced back strong in Game 2. Houston had to meet force with force in order to get that second game, with Olajuwon providing most of the muscle.

Veteran Rolando Blackman isn't in the Knicks' rotation these days, but he knows the game. Blackman is convinced New York can win this series.

"We ran our plays and got the shots we wanted," Blackman said. "They just didn't fall tonight. I've seen John Starks have off-games like this before, and I guarantee he will come back stronger than ever."

The Rockets will have to play better to win Game 2.

I wonder if they fully understand that.

June 9

At practice today, it didn't take long to realize that the national media hadn't been pleased with the aesthetics of last night's game.

Maybe the journalists still haven't accepted the idea of an NBA Finals without Michael Jordan. Maybe they find defense boring. Or maybe, like Wally Matthews, they're just cranky from having to deal with the Houston heat.

Everybody seemed to be talking about what an ugly game it had been. Houston's offense was bad; New York's offense was worse.

Are they the New York Knicks or the New York Bricks?

Chuck Daly, the New Jersey coach who's analyzing The Finals for a New York television station, delivered a dissertation on this subject as reporters milled around looking for material to explain the dearth of scoring.

"The NBA, right now, is an 80-point game," Daly said. "I'd like to see the exploration of some rule changes, so we can put the basket back in basketball."

Strange that Daly would talk about rule changes now. He didn't seem to mind low-scoring games when the Bad Boys from Detroit were winning titles.

Tomjanovich is making no apologies for winning 85–78, and Riley is making no apologies for losing 85–78.

"Blame that guy over there," Riley said, pointing at Daly.

"The league as a whole is much more defensive oriented than it was in the early 1980s. When Detroit won championships with that defensive mentality and Chicago won with that defensive mentality—even though they had the greatest player in the game—other teams began to model themselves that way."

I think this negative perspective on "Uglyball" is unfair. You're talking about two outstanding defensive teams in this series, featuring two of the top shot-blockers in the league. Who cares if the winning team scores 100 points?

If you want a 130–129 game, go to the downtown YMCA.

"With these two teams, defensive is always going to rule," Dawson said. "That's how the Knicks got here; that's how we got here.

"But will the shooting marks stay *that* far down? I wouldn't think so. Keep in mind that the Knicks were coming off a tight, tough series. They had to be a little weary. We were rusty after having not played in a week. Plus, you factor in the tightness and nervousness of a Game 1 in The Finals. Things are going to loosen up."

So far, the Rockets seem to be handling the media crunch pretty well. But I know that as this series wears on, these players are going to feel the heat and the pressure like never before.

There are basically two types of stories in The Finals: Hero stories and goat stories. If your team won the last game, you're OK. If not, the media will pick out the primary culprits in a hurry.

Some players will be able to deal with the media scrutiny; some will struggle with the head games.

In 1986, Lewis Lloyd had a tremendous year for the Rockets right through the Western Conference Finals. But Lloyd got off to a poor start in The Finals against Boston, and the media went after him. Lloyd's problems snowballed to the point where poor Lew was totally bereft of confidence by the end of the series.

The guy feeling the media heat today is John Starks.

If he's mentally tough, he'll come out smoking tomorrow night and get everybody off his back.

June 10

When the Dallas Mavericks traded Derek Harper to the Knicks in early January, the Rockets were leading the cheers. They wanted this longtime Rocket killer out of their division and out of their conference.

But after what happened tonight, Houston wishes Harper had stayed a Texan. Harper was the X-factor as the Knicks stunned the Rockets 91–83 at The Summit and at least temporarily snatched away the home-court advantage.

Who says the Knicks can't shoot straight?

Harper popped in 18 points, including four of six three-pointers. Starks bounced back from his Game 1 nightmare to score 19 points. The Knicks shot .522 from the floor, blocked 10 shots and romped off the court content in the knowledge that the series is being played on their methodical terms.

Don't look now, but the Rockets are in the somewhat tenuous position of knowing they have to win at least one of three in New York to stay alive.

"The 2-3-2 format, it's like hara-kiri," Riley said. "There's no guarantee. We probably woke the Houston Rockets up. The playoffs don't get interesting until the home team loses a game."

The Rockets have been so good in the clutch lately, I thought they would pull it out despite a third-period malaise that put them in a seven-point hole entering the final quarter.

But Harper came up huge at crunch time. With Houston leading 79–78 at the 4:23 mark, he hit a trey to give the Knicks the lead for good. Then, at the two-minute mark, Harper struck again with a three-pointer that made it 87–81.

"Derek did not hesitate tonight," Riley said. "That rim has to look like the ocean. He stepped right into his shot."

While Harper and Starks were flourishing, Smith and Maxwell hit the skids. Smith seems reluctant to drive and can't get open looks from the perimeter because the Knicks aren't leaving the outside people to double team Olajuwon.

Smith hit only 1 of 6 shots and is 2 of 10 in the series. Cassell was 2 of 8 and Maxwell—while scoring 20 points—finished Game 2 with seven turnovers.

"I don't feel we were ready for what they threw at us," Tomjanovich said. "We're backed into a corner now, but this team seems to respond best in that situation."

The Rockets realize they've got a tough series on their hands now. But they don't seem intimidated by the prospects of playing three consecutive games at Madison Square Garden.

Since the NBA went to the 2-3-2 Finals format in '84–'85, the home team has never swept the middle three games.

It's time for concern—but not panic.

"I don't see any team beating us three in a row, even on the road," Maxwell said.

Tomjanovich decided to bring Bullard out of the mothballs for tonight's game. At 6–10, he has the height to match up at small forward with the likes of Charles Smith. It was hoped that Bullard's outside shooting touch would boost the struggling Houston offense.

But Bullard hit only 1 of 7 shots. Meanwhile, Herrera and Elie expressed frustration with their playing stints—seven minutes apiece.

Before tonight's revolting turnaround, the Rockets had been on a two-week magic carpet ride. They had won the last two games of the Utah series, enjoyed a week of adulation and then won the series opener against the Knicks.

There was bound to be a serious roadblock sooner or later.

Sometimes, reality hurts.

June 11

On an early-morning flight from Houston to New York, with a connection in Cincinnati, you either do a lot of thinking or a lot of sleeping.

I couldn't sleep.

My first thought dealt with a possible resumption of the Kenny Smith soap opera.

If history has taught us anything this year, it's that Smith's name always comes up when the Rocket ship experiences turbulence. Because Harper had his way with Smith in Game 2 and because Smith has only five points in this series, the pressure will be on Kenny tomorrow as he takes the court in his hometown.

As the teams head for Manhattan, I'm wondering whether Smith will bounce back in good shape. The officials are allowing Harper to fend off Smith with powerful handchecks as Smith advances the ball. Cassell is much stronger than Smith and therefore can deal with the handchecks more successfully.

But how much can a coach rely on a rookie point guard in a championship series? At some point, Smith will have to come through if Houston is to prevail in this series.

"The first goal is to get in the right frame of mind," Smith said. "The second is to have the ability to see what your strengths are and utilize them. My strength is my shooting ability, and I haven't utilized it."

If Smith doesn't get it going tomorrow, the New York media will be all over him like so many amateur psychologists.

My second thought is that Olajuwon is hesitating too much when he makes his move against single coverage. Too many times in the opening two games, Hakeem has been caught between shot and pass.

The Knicks, with Anthony Mason getting much of the credit, have been able to limit Olajuwon to 1-of-8 shooting in the fourth quarters. If Hakeem will just make his move and fire away, New York won't have a consistent defensive answer.

My final thought (three thoughts constitute my limit for one morning) deals with the Rockets' ability to handle this crazy environment called New York City. There's so much going on in this concrete jungle. Everything seems faster. Everything seems magnified.

The club is going to be here for a week, and that's more than enough time to lose focus.

What is it Frank Sinatra croons about New York? If you can make it there, you can make it anywhere.

June 12

With one flick of his right wrist, Sam "I Am" Cassell has become an overnight national celebrity.

If the Rockets go on to win the world championship, everyone will surely think back to Cassell's clutch bomb that turned defeat into victory in Game 3. Just call it the shot heard 'round Houston.

Doesn't this kid know the meaning of the word pressure?

The Knicks had stormed back from a 14-point deficit at the 7:42 mark of the third quarter to take an 88–86 lead on Harper's jumper with 52 seconds remaining.

The noise in Madison Square Garden was deafening as the Rockets worked the ball to Olajuwon. Hakeem went into his move and was about to shoot when he noticed Cassell's man had drifted away. Olajuwon sent the ball to Cassell, who was beyond the three-point line deep down the middle.

The rookie never hesitated. He jumped and shot in a fluid manner. The ball seemed to hang in the air for an eternity before landing in the bottom of the net.

"Sam Cassell . . . from *downtown*," shouted an impressed Marv Albert, the NBC telecaster.

Albert is also the longtime voice of the New York Knicks. He knows that visiting players—especially rookies—are not expected to defy the magic of Madison Square Garden in championship moments.

My mind flashed to the first conversation I had with Cassell, way back in fall training camp. I had asked him about guarding Anfernee Hardaway and Cassell had reminded me Hardaway would have to guard him, too.

It was that kind of inner confidence that enabled Cassell to win Game 3 for the Rockets with a three-pointer that will be frozen in time.

"Sam Cassell," marveled Tomjanovich, "is one courageous player."

Cassell's monster shot gave Houston an 89–88 lead with 32 seconds remaining. When Ewing set a blatant moving pick on Maxwell while trying to free Starks for a winning shot, official Jake O'Donnell made the gutsy call. Cassell then cinched it with four free throws, as the Knicks were forced to foul to stop the clock.

Rockets 93, Knicks 89. In the postgame interviews, Cassell's ice-water veins became the dominant theme.

"I wasn't comfortable going up with a jump hook," Olajuwon said. "I wanted three in that situation, not two. Sam is a gambler. I think he plays a lot of street basketball, plays in the park, so I think he is an experienced player, not a rookie. He makes big shots like it is no big deal. Well, this was a very big deal."

You've got that right, Hakeem. The Rockets, with a 2–1 series lead, will not lose this series at Madison Square Garden. The big picture ramification is that if the Knicks are to win the title, they'll have to do it in The Summit.

Cassell acted like it was just another game back on the Baltimore playgrounds, where he grew up.

"Dream created it all," Cassell said. "He made the pass and I made the shot."

Oh, if only it were that simple.

Someday, Cassell may wake up and realize his three-pointer to win Game 3 was the single most important shot in Rockets history.

"Trey" it again, Sam.

June 13

It's getting big now.

So big that Olajuwon is appearing on *The Late Show With David Letterman.* So big that the world-famous Carnegie Deli in midtown Manhattan has dreamed up a two-pound sandwich in honor of the Rockets MVP center.

The "Hakeem The Dream" sandwich contains corned beef, pastrami, turkey, beef brisket, Swiss cheese, cole slaw, pickles and a hot pepper. Cost: $15.95. And don't forget the $3 charge for sharing.

The sandwich has a little bit of everything, just like Olajuwon's game, according to Murray Trachtenberg, the deli's general manager.

Hakeem didn't have a chance to try the sandwich today. He was a couple of blocks away from the deli, going one-on-one with Letterman.

I watched the show in my hotel room and thought Hakeem came through remarkably well. Letterman put away his biting wit shortly after Olajuwon said it was an "honor" to be with Letterman. That's what you call softening up the opponent.

Olajuwon drew laughs by explaining how he wound up playing for the University of Houston instead of St. John's in New York.

"New York was too cold, that's all," Olajuwon said.

Olajuwon said his parents had never seen him play in person.

"I send videotapes to Nigeria. All of them are the games we won. To my family, I have been the MVP for a long time," Olajuwon said.

"So your parents think you're undefeated?" Letterman asked.

"They did . . . until they got CNN," Olajuwon laughed.

It was a good day for all of the Rockets to get away from the pressures of the series and have some fun. Many of the players had dinner and went to jazz clubs for a little relaxation.

Houston is on firm footing with a 2–1 series lead. And if the Rockets can just get one of the next two in New York, they'll have a toehold.

While the Rockets cavorted today, the Knicks were seething.

Riley was extremely displeased with his team's start in Game 3. Houston burst to a 42–26 lead in the opening 18 minutes.

"They kicked our ass at the beginning of the game by establishing their aggression," Riley said. "We can't put ourselves in a position of having to dodge bullets and hit home runs at the end.

"I wish we could play again right now. The worst thing is having two days off between games. I've got to sit around and read all this crap."

Testy, testy.

I think Riley is deliberately creating a mood today. I think his biggest goal is to make sure his team plays with a major chip on its shoulder right from the start in Game 4.

The Knicks aren't out of this series by a long shot. If they win the next two at home, they will have two chances to wrap it up in Houston. Because the Knicks already have won once at The Summit, they should have confidence if it comes down to winning one more on the road.

Never count out the two Pats—Riley and Ewing.

They're capable of having sandwiches named after them, too.

June 14

In a championship series, there are two primary buzzwords: "choke" and "guarantee."

Hakeem used the former word in an off-handed manner, and a few media people are trying to make a big deal out of it.

After the Rockets took a 2–1 series lead, Olajuwon said in a television interview: "If we go up 3–1, they will choke."

First of all, a team can't choke being down 1–3. The connotation of the word "choke" is being up and letting it get away. As in Choke City, when the Rockets were up 20 and lost to Phoenix.

But nobody stopped to think about logic.

If the word "choke" is used in any form or fashion, the impulse of the media is to throw it out there and hope the other team will respond, thus creating a bulletin-board war of words.

It's a silly little media game that is being played today, with Olajuwon being asked to explain the "choke" comment.

"It's nothing against the Knicks," Olajuwon said. "I don't want that to be misunderstood. I'm not trying to provoke controversy."

Olajuwon explained that he was simply trying to say a 3–1 deficit for the Knicks would be nearly impossible to overcome because it would require two more road victories.

"Their chances would be like making a shot from half court," Olajuwon said.

Thanks, Hakeem. I'm sure everybody back in Houston feels much better now that the ChokeGate case has been closed.

Here in New York, nobody really cares.

Everybody is ecstatic about the New York Rangers winning the Stanley Cup tonight and ending a 54-year championship drought.

I went outside the New York Hilton after the hockey game to get a sense of the city's celebratory mood. People were driving through Manhattan even faster than usual, and the blaring of horns was even noisier than usual.

"Rangers, Rangers, Rangers," one man screamed, as he leaned out of the car window, waving a Rangers' pennant.

This championship revelry looks like fun stuff.

Could it be that the good times will roll in Houston before long?

June 15

When he was coaching the Showtime Lakers, Riley used to say "no rebounds, no rings."

If Riley didn't copyright that phrase, Tomjanovich ought to borrow it. The Rockets lost Game 4 because they didn't rebound. The fired-up Knicks evened the championship series 2–2 with a 91–82 victory, using a 50–33 advantage on the glass as the foundation for success.

"They seemed to want it a little more than we did," Tomjanovich said. "We didn't match their intensity tonight. New York is the No. 1 rebounding team in the league, and they showed us why."

The tone was set right away because the Knicks were almost as aggressive as a Central Park mugger. New York missed its first shot, but Oakley muscled in for an offensive rebound. The Knicks missed again, and Harper claimed the offensive rebound, sending Tomjanovich into a sideline stomping session.

The Knicks went on to mount a 17–2 lead, and New York fans from Madonna to Woody Allen were on their feet.

Although Olajuwon exploded offensively for the first time in the series to boost Houston to a 56–50 lead in the second half, the uphill climb took its toll on the Rockets. When the high-flying Horry had a crash landing and had to sit out much of the fourth quarter, New York regained control with relentless offensive rebounding.

Horry went soaring to the basket with abandon, but was bumped while in flight by Mason. Horry landed hard on his tailbone. He tried to come back after a brief rest, but the pain was too intense.

No Horry, no chance.

If it turns out that Horry can't play the remainder of this series, the Knicks may as well order the champagne.

"Hopefully, everything will be OK," Horry said. "I've got a sore lower back, a sore left hand and a sore right hand. It was just a hard foul on Mason's part. Those things happen."

With Horry out and Thorpe in foul trouble, the Knicks had 21 offensive rebounds. Playing on a sore ankle, Oakley finished with 16 points and 20 rebounds, including nine on the offensive glass.

There were other disturbing developments for the Rockets, as well. The Smith-Harper matchup is turning into a real dilemma. Smith picked up two early fouls, and Tomjanovich wound up using him only 19 minutes. Harper outscored Smith 21–0, and Starks scored 10 of his 20 points in the last 3:39 to put the Rockets away.

"We got great, great guard play," Riley said.

One truth is becoming self-evident now that this series has been reduced to a best-of-three affair: The Rockets are not going to be able to exploit their speed advantage because they simply can't dictate a fast-tempo game.

New York won't let the Rockets run.

The Knicks go after every rebound like a hungry dog goes after raw meat. Without the crisp rebound and outlet pass, running opportunities are diminished. Furthermore, New York gets stellar defensive play from the backcourt unit of Harper, Starks and Greg Anthony.

The Knicks' guards provide ball pressure and run back defensively with tremendous effort. Riley has them trained in how not to give up easy transition points.

If the Rockets are going to win a championship, they will have to do it on New York's terms.

There won't be any breakdancing. This series is strictly a waltz.

June 16

This series is tied 2–2, but the way people are acting and talking today, you'd think the Knicks are up 3-0.

Horry is banged up, Smith is catching hell from the New York papers, Elie is bemoaning his lack of playing time and Cassell is being romantically linked to Madonna.

The Knicks seemed considerably less fragile when the media visited them after practice. I walked from player to player and observed the confident expressions and statements.

Harper drew a big audience. After a subpar Game 1, he has been sensational in his last three outings. He is averaging 17.0 points and shooting 51 percent in the series, compared to Smith's 3.8 points and .263 field-goal mark.

Reasons? Explanations?

"I just feel he (Smith) is one of those guys who doesn't like ball pressure," Harper said. "It bothers him. But at the same time, I know he's the guy who can make a difference if you give him breathing room. I'm going to stay on him."

Ewing hasn't shot well, but his defensive work and rebounding have been excellent. While Olajuwon has been doing interviews with the likes of Letterman and PBS host Charlie Rose this week, the New York center has preferred to stay out of the limelight.

"I'm going to wait until we win the championship," Ewing said, "to do all of that stuff."

Back at the Rockets' practice headquarters, the good news was that Horry's tailbone X-rays came back negative. Horry proclaimed himself "98 percent."

I wonder if Smith is going to 98 percent from a mental standpoint.

The tabloids here are suggesting Smith is through for the series. They say his confidence is completely shot after Cassell got all the crunch-time minutes in Game 4.

This mini-crisis with Smith is starting the snowball. Will he crater under the media heat like Lew Lloyd did in '86?

Maxwell even said today he is making it a point to get in Smith's ear and encourage his backcourt buddy to "play wild and crazy . . . like me. I personally think we need Kenny to play well to win."

As for the rumored Cassell-Madonna night on the town, Sam is sorry to report the story is a fabrication. They met, he said, but that was all.

"We said hello, goodbye and that was the end of it," Cassell said.

It's a sign of the times, I guess: Over the last few days, the Rockets have been coming up empty in just about every category.

June 17

Basketball had seemed so important for so long.

But during a portion of Game 5—the biggest game of the Rockets' season so far—basketball suddenly didn't seem important at all. I had to write about Houston's 91–84 loss to the Knicks, but my mind kept wandering to the eerie O.J. Simpson highway drama that unfolded on television sets throughout the media headquarters at Madison Square Garden.

Reporters on tight deadlines often watch the second half of Finals games on television from the media room, where they have better access to telephones, electric power and statistical information. When NBC cut away from the game to show the Simpson chase scene, only those media members from Houston and New York voiced objections.

"We've still got a *job* to do," one New York writer shouted.

Because the life-or-death Simpson saga was so gripping, I couldn't totally focus on the game until the final three minutes. That happened to be the time when the issue was decided. With the Rockets leading 80–78 at the 3:12 mark, Smith drove for the basket but lost the ball on the end line.

Starks then drove a stake through Houston's heart by boldly drilling a three-pointer to put the Knicks ahead 81–80 at the 2:22

mark. Smith missed a jumper and Herrera rebounded. But when Herrera tried a putback, Ewing sprang into action with a blocked shot.

Harper leaked out for a breakaway and wound up with two free throws to make it 83–80. When Horry hurriedly missed a three-pointer and Mason snuck away for a layup, it was 85–80 and the Knicks could sense their Uglyball style had them one win away from a title.

The "Starks Reality" is this: Houston must beat New York twice at The Summit or see its championship dream slip away.

The Garden was a madhouse as the final seconds ticked down. Three nights earlier, the Rangers had won a world championship in this building. Now, the New York crazies were anticipating another championship parade.

When the door to the Rockets' locker room opened after the mandatory 10-minute cooling off period, Horry was quick to reassure Rockets fans the championship dream is still very much alive because of the home-court factor.

"We aren't going to lose," Horry declared. "We have two wins in us. No doubt about it. We'll have our fans behind us, and we're going to get it done."

Once again, the Knicks guards got the best of the Houston guards. Starks and Harper outscored Maxwell and Smith 33–14. Mason had a huge game off the bench with 17 points and nine rebounds, and Horry—still shaking off the effects of his frightening fall in Game 4—hit only 2 of 14 shots.

I'll give the Rockets credit for this: They're sticking together at a time when it would be easy to point fingers in the direction of the guy at the next locker.

Asked if he was "concerned" about the play of the Houston backcourt, Olajuwon refused to take the media bait.

"We are a team," Olajuwon said emphatically. "We don't separate the guards, the forwards or the centers. The games have been so close. They could have gone either way. When it is like that, the difference is home-court advantage."

It was late when we wrapped up our stories and walked out to the intersection of 33rd Street and Eighth Avenue.

So long, Madison Square Garden.

Tomorrow, we head back to Houston, where the true character of the '93–'94 Rockets will be measured.

I wonder what the Houston fans are thinking after two frustrating endings at the Garden. Could it be: "Here we go again?"

June 18

Manhattan almost seems like a normal place at 5:30 a.m.

The Houston Post's army of reporters took the milk run back to Texas. Since the Rockets are not practicing today, the only way we can get interviews is to beat the team home and wait on its charter to arrive at Hobby Airport.

When the plane taxied in, only the front-office staff immediately exited.

The players stayed on board for a team meeting. When they finally filed off the plane, the mood was upbeat.

"We are in the driver's seat, even though we're down 3–2," Olajuwon shouted above the roar of the plane's engine. "We lost the home-court advantage, but then we gained it back."

If the Rockets are in the driver's seat, as Olajuwon claims, they'd better fasten their seat belts. It figures to be a bumpy ride from here on out.

I looked around for Tomjanovich, but he had already headed for his red Jeep and was about to drive back toward the plane to load his baggage. I stopped Rudy en route.

He seemed convinced the Rockets could end this season in story-book fashion.

"If somebody would have told me way back when that we could become world champions by winning our last two games of the season . . . you'd take that," Tomjanovich said.

I asked Tomjanovich about the context of the team meeting on the plane.

"Our guys tried to put it in perspective," Tomjanovich said. "We went to New York having lost the home-court advantage, and we came back with the home-court advantage. The opportunity is there."

Will being home make that much difference? Already, there are signs that it might.

As Tomjanovich was speaking, he glanced beyond a fence at a huge throng of Rockets fans who had come to the airport on a Saturday afternoon—following two tough losses—to welcome the team home and say they still believe in the dream.

"That," Tomjanovich said softly, "is great. It was just what we needed."

One thing Rudy will preach tomorrow is for the players to concentrate on getting back defensively. One or two easy scores in a series this tight can mean the difference between victory and defeat.

Tomjanovich said the Rockets can't afford to let the frustration of a missed shot or a blocked shot detract from their commitment to prevent breakaways by the Knicks.

"I really feel that element cost us Game 2 and Game 5," he said. "In Game 4, the big problem was rebounding. You can talk about all the little subplots. But that's where it's really at. Every point is crucial, and we just can't allow those easy baskets."

Just after the Rockets had loaded their bags and driven away, the dark clouds gave way to a driving rainstorm at Hobby Airport.

It was raining so hard, I could hardly see to walk to my car.

If the Rockets expect to win a world championship, they had better be as angry as today's weather.

June 19

Dream on, Houston.

After eight preseason games, 82 regular-season games and 22 playoff games, the Rockets are going to lace up their sneakers one last time and compete for the championship of the basketball world.

Houston forced Game 7 by edging the Knicks 86–84 today. And when I say *edging,* I mean it. If Olajuwon doesn't get his fingertips on a last-gasp bomb by a red-hot Starks, this city might well be in deep mourning right now.

I had seen this situation last year in Game 6 of the Phoenix-Chicago Final: With a 3–2 lead in the series, the road team has the ball for a last shot, trailing by two. Last year, John Paxson reared up for a three-pointer to win the title for the Bulls.

This time, it was another John going for the win from three-point range in Game 6. But John Starks didn't account for the league's Defensive Player of the Year roaring in his direction. Just as Starks veered left after getting a pick from Ewing, Olajuwon lunged from nowhere to barely tip the shot as it left Starks' hand.

The ball fluttered down well short of the basket, and Thorpe tipped it toward the corner as the buzzer sounded. Tomjanovich thrust his right fist into the air and galloped triumphantly to the locker room.

Riley wiped his forehead and walked toward the tunnel, no doubt wondering if the Knicks had wasted their best chance to win this series.

Wasn't it inevitable that this tight, tense series should come down to a Game 7? The Rockets and Knicks will do it once more, with feeling.

I watched the nail-biting finish from the press room. _Houston Post_ columnist Mickey Herskowitz was standing alongside and questioned whether Olajuwon had caught Starks on the hand as the all-or-nothing bomb was released.

A few minutes later, I asked NBC's Matt Guokas, who had seen several replays. No foul, said Guokas.

This is the simple essence of what winning a championship is all about.

It's about a great player digging deep within himself to summon that last bit of energy he didn't know he had. It's about an Olajuwon playing 43 minutes, scoring 30 points and still demanding that his heavy legs carry him to the three-point line in an instant when the smell of defeat is in the air.

Starks had been sensational with 16 points in the fourth quarter. There's no doubt in my mind that if Olajuwon doesn't get to the ball, the Knicks are the champions.

"You saw why Hakeem is the Defensive Player of the Year," Elie said. "He's just so quick."

Olajuwon said he didn't realize Starks had set up behind the three-point line. Hakeem shook his head and laughed when somebody told him Starks had been going for broke.

"Oh, man, he has no conscience."

Then Olajuwon had an important afterthought.

"I'm just glad that Ewing was setting the pick . . . so I could get there," Olajuwon said. "It took everything I had to make that stretch."

If he had it to do over, I'll bet Riley would use a power forward to set the pick for Starks—with Ewing taking Olajuwon as far away from the play as possible.

Sorry, Pat. I realize hindsight is 20–20.

"Hakeem just kept making play after play," Oakley said. "He fought us off all day."

Olajuwon had the necessary help from his friends. Smith lifted a grand piano off his back with his first big shot of the series—a three-pointer that pushed Houston up 84–77 at the 3:17 mark. Herrera enabled Houston to overcome a shaky start by hitting 6 of 6 shots in a masterful performance coming off the bench.

Herrera is turning into a major story. Recruited diligently by scout John Killilea a few years ago, Herrera joined the Rockets after starting his pro career in Spain. Last year, the University of Houston product was solid in the regular season but flopped in the playoffs because of fatigue.

Maybe that shoulder injury Herrera suffered in the Phoenix series was a blessing in disguise.

He has come back in The Finals with fresh legs, saving the Rockets in Games 1 and 6.

Now, it's T-minus 48 minutes until glory.

"You can't ask for a better situation than to play one game for the championship on your home court," Olajuwon said. "I'm so happy we have put ourselves in that position. But now, we have to complete the mission."

History is on the Rockets' side.

Everybody will point out that stat about the home team not having lost a Game 7 since '82. And the long delay between Games 6 and 7 could work in Houston's favor. The Knicks must stay in a hotel during the Sunday night to Wednesday night wait while the Rockets resume a normal home routine.

Somebody measure Olajuwon's fingertips. That could be the margin of victory if, in fact, the Rockets go on to claim the title.

One . . . more . . . win.

As I drive alongside Westheimer this morning, reading all those marquee signs supporting the Rockets, it boggles my mind to contemplate what one more win would mean to people in this city.

It won't reduce a Houstonian's tax bill. It won't mean Houston is suddenly going to have 72-degree days in July and August.

But it *will* lift the spirit of Houstonians from all walks of life. It *will* make Houstonians speak of their city with more pride. It *will* drive away that inferiority complex that has haunted Houston sports fans who want—just once—to say they live in a city of champions.

If the Rockets win, I'll be happy for the city in general and happy for certain individuals, in particular, who have given so much to the Rockets organization over the years.

Topping that list is Ray Patterson, the true patriarch of this franchise. If Ray hadn't kept the club afloat through the club's financially strained early years in Houston, this city wouldn't be on the verge of having a world championship celebration.

This one's for you, Ray.

Steve Patterson can also bask in the glow of a championship if the Rockets win one more ballgame. Steve was at the general manager controls when the personality of this Rockets' club was being defined. It's Steve's team as much as it is Rudy's.

It's also your team, Charlie Thomas. In 11 years as the Rockets owner, you ran the organization with a good head and a good heart. The decision to start from scratch with an ambitious rebuilding program in 1982 ultimately resulted in the Rockets putting together a ballclub around Olajuwon. And the decision by Thomas to make Tomjanovich the permanent head coach before the '92–'93 season ranks as one of the most astute moves in franchise history.

There are many other special people who come to mind because their lives have been intertwined with the Rockets organization over the course of many seasons. I think about Calvin Murphy, Mike Newlin, Gene Peterson, Jim Foley and statistician Mike Davitt. I think about Bill Worrell who—unlike many of us transplanted Houstonians—has waited for this kind of championship moment his entire life. I think about how much Dr. Charles Baker—the club's primary physician from 1972 through last year—loved the Rockets.

I think about Concetta Vandervoort, the wife of the late Rockets trainer Dick Vandervoort. I still see her in the stands at virtually every home game.

Concetta, Game 7 is for you, too.

If the Rockets win, I'll be happy for David Nordstrom, the team's longtime equipment manager and for Ed Bernholz, a retired businessman who works for the Rockets on a volunteer basis simply because he loves the game and the people in it.

I'll also be happy for Jim Boylen and Robert Barr—two young members of Tomjanovich's staff who have made vital contributions to the success of the program.

In one way or another, all of the aforementioned people have enhanced the fabric of the Rockets organization.

One . . . more . . . win.

It would mean so much to so many.

June 21

Those of us in the media often have a tendency to overhype sporting events. Today, that's impossible.

It is as though this city is in a collective trance. Rockets versus Knicks. Game 7. For everything.

Russ Small, Charlie Palillo, Rich Lord and the gang over at the Rockets' flagship station KTRH, probably have the best handle on the mood of Houston because they talk with the fans on a daily basis.

"No doubt, it is no contest, this is the biggest and greatest and most anticipated sporting event in the history of this city," Palillo said. "If the city wins, it is going be like the world's largest pressure release valve has been opened up."

Yeah, and if the city loses, it's going to be the Great Depression, Part II.

There will be horrible reruns of the tortured moments in Houston sports history: Nolan Ryan and Bob Knepper failing to hold late three-run leads with the World Series so tantalizingly close; Mike Renfro making a great touchdown catch in Pittsburgh and having it taken away by an erring official; Lorenzo Charles dunking the game-winner at the buzzer for North Carolina State; and Larry Bird drilling the clutch three-pointers when the Rockets crept within range of a title.

"Just once, let Houston have more confetti in the air than mosquitoes," wrote *The Houston Post*'s Kenny Hand. "Just once, let Houston have a world championship banner to hang."

I made the rounds at practice one last time. Tomorrow will be game No. 113, counting preseason, regular season and playoffs. The other 112 games suddenly seem irrelevant.

What have you done lately?

There have been nine months worth of sweat and tears, and it all comes down to 48 telling minutes on the second night of summer.

Rudy seemed at ease as he addressed the media. He was talking about his superstition ace in the hole.

"I haven't lost with my black suit, and I've probably worn it about 10 times," Tomjanovich said. "I wore it in Game 3 in New York and I thought about wearing it again the next game, but you can't push the gods too hard, so I didn't."

Rest assured, that black suit will be worn by Tomjanovich tomorrow. You don't save anything at this point.

Across the way, Hakeem was trying to remind everybody that it's still just a basketball game, not a world war. He put it in perspective by talking about a recent visit he had with a boy who has leukemia.

"That reminds you of what's important," Olajuwon said. "Just to be able to run up and down, you give thanks for that."

Olajuwon said the key is for the Rockets to savor the competition.

"It's a championship game, and we must enjoy having the opportunity to play in it," Olajuwon said. "You can't make it out to be so big that you're afraid to take the shot and play your normal game."

I listened to a few more conversations and then went back to the press room to write my last advance story of the season. The quote that was uppermost in my mind had come from Kenny Smith.

"When we win this game," Smith had said, "it will change our lives forever."

Indeed, careers are about to be defined by what happens tomorrow on a 94-foot piece of hardwood. If the Rockets come out on top, they will have won an everlasting place in the hearts of Houstonians.

"One more win would make it a dream season," Olajuwon had said. "I'm hoping."

So is every Rockets fan.

June 22

Live the dream, Houstonians. Pinch yourselves seven times and let the two most glorious words in a sports fan's vocabulary roll smoothly off your tongue again and again.

World Champions! Yes, your Rockets are the 1994 world champions.

Choke City is out, Champ City is in.

Finally, it is over. Finally, the dream is real. Hakeem Olajuwon— who else?—carried the Rockets to a 90–84 series-clinching victory over New York Wednesday night, and it was like Mardi Gras and New Year's Eve had been rolled into one giant celebration.

When the buzzer sounded, pandemonium reigned. Players and coaches ran amok, looking for people to hug. Tears of joy were everywhere as fans rocked The Summit to its foundation.

Live the dream, Houston. World champions.

No more inferiority complex for Sam Houston's town. The scoreboard numbers glowed radiantly as decades of pro sports frustration were swept away in one thrilling, dramatic, unforgettable evening.

Live the dream, Houston. World champions.

Of the 1,500 or so Rockets game-story leads that I have sent into *The Houston Post* computer the last 15 years, this is the one that gives me the most satisfaction.

I have been taught to be a detached, neutral journalist, not a flag-waving supporter of the home club. But while I'm not part of the team, I *am* part of the city.

You'd have to be a pretty hard-bitten member of the community not to enjoy what's happening in Houston, Texas, on this night.

This town has exploded with happiness because—for the first time in history—its citizens can raise their index fingers and shout about being undisputed No. 1 in a major pro sport. Houston may go on to win 50 more world championships, but there can never be another spontaneous outpouring of emotion like this, simply because there's something pure and magical about a first Titletown experience.

I watched the second half on television from the press room. The Rockets had maintained a narrow lead after wiping out a 25–22 Knicks lead early in the second quarter with a 7–0 run.

New York, however, just wouldn't go away.

The Rockets led only 78–75 with 2:51 remaining. A couple of stops, a couple of hoops and the Knicks could have carted that world championship trophy back to New York.

But Olajuwon dropped in a jump hook and the Knicks couldn't answer on the ensuing possession. Who would deliver the knockout punch?

None other than Mad Max.

With the shot clock running down, Olajuwon went into his move, made the defense commit and then spotted Maxwell open on the left wing. There was no time to think. Maxwell squared his shoulders and stepped into the shot with a smooth release.

Nothing but net. Nothing but ecstacy in The Summit. The three-pointer gave Houston an 83–75 lead at the 1:49 mark, and the Rockets could sense that Houston was about to become Champ City.

Maxwell trotted back on defense and then suddenly leaped into the air with a show of pure joy.

Maxwell knew. Everybody knew. After a nine-month quest that began in a stuffy Galveston high school gym on Oct. 7, the Rockets had become the best basketball team in the world.

"No question about it . . . that was the biggest shot of my career," Maxwell would later say. "I don't dream too much, but that shot . . . it was big."

There were 4.2 seconds remaining when two Maxwell free throws made it a six-point game. Celebrations had already begun. New York threw a long pass and the Rockets intercepted, with Olajuwon—so fittingly—dribbling the ball as the clock hit 0:00.

Rather than diving into the courtside sea of humanity, I waited in the press room and watched NBC's poignant pictures of the trophy presentation. There was Rudy hugging wife Sophie; there was Hakeem, floating back from the madness to reflect on the scene and enjoy the joy of others.

"Houston . . . you wanted it so long," Tomjanovich said. "You've finally got it. I'm proud to be part of the team that got it for us. And when I say team, I mean it in the truest sense of the word."

At that point, I headed for the Rockets' locker room. There were people inside the jam-packed room I had never seen. Players? Where were the players?

Jim Boylen poured cold champagne on my head and I wound up with a soggy notebook.

Oh, well. Didn't look like I'd be using it, anyway.

Finally, the champagne party lessened in its intensity, and the guys who made it happen were asked to put these golden moments in perspective.

"It feels 20 times better than I ever thought it could," said Smith, who withstood the media heat to make key contributions in Games 6 and 7. "We hung together as a team. There was never a doubt we were going to get it done."

Horry, Thorpe, Herrera and Cassell were gallant in Game 7. And Olajuwon was Olajuwon.

"When they flew that championship trophy to Houston, that was motivation," Olajuwon said. "I thought, 'how can they bring this trophy to Houston—we want it more than any other city—and then fly it out of Houston . . . to New York?' It would have been a disaster. I can't even picture that.

"I was more concerned about that than the championship itself. At that point, it wasn't about the championship. It was about pride. It was about us not allowing them to take that trophy out of our building and our city. If they had celebrated on our court, that would have hurt me more than losing the championship."

In the Knicks' locker room, there was utter despair. Starks, who had been so brilliant in Game 6, suffered through a nightmarish 2 of 18 shooting performance, including 0 for 11 from three-point range.

Ewing appeared to be in a daze as he left The Summit. The Knicks have a lot of older players. Will New York's valiant warrior ever get this close to a championship ring again? Maybe, maybe not.

Pat Riley? He has often said there are only two things in the NBA: Winning and misery. He feels miserable tonight but was gracious in defeat.

"We got beat by a hell of a basketball team," he said.

It was very late when I walked out of The Summit and made the short drive to *The Houston Post*. Early in the evening, the newspaper had two front-page headlines in mind.

Option No. 1: "Champ City!"

Option No. 2: "Heartbreak!"

I looked at the front page. "Champ City!" it was.

I just wanted to make sure of the tangible evidence.

It was the wee hours now. I walked to my car and began the 12-mile drive home. Horns were blaring and people were shouting as though it were midnight on New Year's Eve.

Only the horns and the shouting didn't stop. I heard noises ring out until I walked into my house and closed the front door at 3 a.m.

All I could think about was what this Houston night would sound like if headline option No. 2 had been used.

The silence, no doubt, would have been deafening.

How could throwing a ball through a hoop make so much difference?

The Houston Rockets had reached out and touched the heart of the nation's fourth-largest city.

Never again will Houston think of itself as a loser.

June 23

It's 6 a.m.

I didn't get much sleep, and I'm still reeking of champagne. But this is as good a time as any to make my final journal entry on the '93–'94 Rockets season. Later today, there will be a press conference in honor of Olajuwon, the NBA Finals MVP. My family and I are going to be among the 50,000 at a Rockets' victory rally tonight, and tomorrow the team will be saluted during a downtown championship parade.

I'd like to discuss last night's championship-clinching win with my 9-year-old son, Joey, who attended the game as an avid Rockets fan. As I look in his room, however, he's still fast asleep.

I'd like to tell him that last night's game will mean even more to him when he's 19 than it does now. And it will mean more to him at 29 than at 19.

For a sports fan, the championship memories always become richer with time.

I'd also like to tell him how lucky he is to be so young and already have a championship to celebrate.

But I can't tell him that right now because he's asleep.

The funny thing is, when he wakes up, he'll still be in Dreamland.

Epilogue

It is June 30, eight days after the most significant event in Houston sports history.

The glow of victory is warm and persistent.

I have seen the world champion Rockets take their bows in the Astrodome and wave to an estimated 500,000 at a downtown parade. Hakeem Olajuwon and Rudy Tomjanovich are now demigods in this city, and the remaining players and coaches have become stars in their own right.

What was it Kenny Smith said on the eve of Game 7 against the Knicks?:

"When we win this game, it will change our lives forever."

That's the basic theme I want to explore with Tomjanovich today as we talk in-depth for the first time since Houston became Title-town, U.S.A. I want to discuss how lives have been changed and how the Rockets must cope with that as they move into a new season cast as the kings of the hill.

We are at Walden on Lake Houston and a golf tournament has just ended.

"Let's go sit over there," said Tomjanovich, pointing out a quiet location.

"As great as all this is, life goes on," I said. "How do you bring everybody back to earth so that you can go after it again?"

Tomjanovich admitted it will be tough to get everybody focused toward a drive for a repeat title.

"To come back and do it again . . . man, that's going to take something," Tomjanovich said. "You talk about fighting human nature. This is the biggest test of all because it's just human nature to feel pretty damn good about yourself.

"I've got so much respect for the Lakers, Pistons and Bulls. They were the champs before us, and each team followed its initial title with a repeat. I think the common denominator is sheer pride. We have to come out with a pride which lets everybody know it's special to be a Rocket. That type of pride can overcome human nature, and that's how you repeat. We're going to be the targeted team now. We have to be hungry and humble. The mindset is so important.

"I love Houston, and I'm so proud of what we did. My players have worked hard for me for two years and all that work paid off. But at some point, you have to move to the next challenge, and we've got a big one in front of us this year.

"A repeat champion is going to be remembered as one of the great teams to come along in the history of the game. It's a unique opportunity to be on top of the hill and fighting to protect your territory.

"To do all of this and then just fall back and let somebody take it from you . . . that would be a shame. We have set our standards high, and we intend to keep them high."

Yes, life goes on.

Another season, another challenge.

Maybe Houston will win another world championship. Or two. Or three.

But there can only be one _first_ championship. And that is why—to Houstonians—there can never be a team as special as the '93–'94 Rockets.

Never.

Index